Silver in My Sporran

BY THE SAME AUTHOR

Adult Fiction
The Painted Doll Affair
The Golden Venus Affair
Duel in Glenfinnan
Maniac
Night on the Killer Reef
The Canisbay Conspiracy
Murder at the Open
The Grey Shepherds
The Hammers of Fingal
The Killings on Kersivay
The Dancing Horse
Escort to Adventure
Fugitive's Road
Greybreek
Death on the Machar
The Crouching Spy
Strangers from the Sea
Eleven for Danger
The Singing Spider
Crime's Masquerader
The Crooked Finger
Flowering Death
The Cavern
The Ten Green Brothers
The Temple Falls
The Screaming Gull
Death by the Mistletoe
The Purple Rock

Plays
Minister's Monday
Stranger at Christmas
Final Proof
Mercy Flight
Storm Tide
Under Suspicion
Murder in Lettermore

Children's Fiction
Super Nova and the Frozen Man
Super Nova and the Rogue Satellite
Life-boat – Green to White
The Kersivay Kraken
The Cave of the Hammers
The High Cliffs of Kersivay
Space Agent and the Ancient Peril
Space Agent and the Isles of Fire
Space Agent from the Lost Planet
Killpatrick, Special Reporter
Satellite 7
The Atom Chasers in Tibet
The Atom Chasers
Dinny Smith Comes Home
Peril on the Lost Planet
Red Fire on the Lost Planet
Secret of the Lost Planet
Return to the Lost Planet
The Lost Planet
Tiger Mountain
The Grey Pilot
Stubby Sees it Through
King Abbie's Adventure
Faraway Island
The Black Wherry
The Crocodile Men

Non Fiction
Rocks in My Scotch
Heather in My Ears
Salt in My Porridge
The Kirk at the Corner
Rescue Call
Let's Visit Scotland

Angus MacVicar

Silver in My Sporran
Confessions of a Writing Man

835447 | 920/MACV.

Hutchinson of London

Hutchinson & Co (Publishers) Ltd
3 Fitzroy Square, London w1p 6jd

London Melbourne Sydney Auckland
Wellington Johannesburg and agencies
throughout the world

First published 1979
© Angus MacVicar 1979

Set in VIP Times

Printed in Great Britain by
The Anchor Press Ltd, and bound by
Wm Brendon & Son Ltd, both of
Tiptree, Essex

British Library Cataloguing in Publication Data
MacVicar, Angus
  Silver in my sporran.
  1. MacVicar, Angus – Biography   2. Authors,
  Scottish – 20th century – Biography
  I. Title
  941.1082′092′4   PR6025.A34Z/

isbn 0 09 136850 2

To encourage
(and entertain)
RONA MUNRO
and other beginning writers

Acknowledgements

For permission to reproduce photographs my grateful thanks
are due to Mr Harry Hodgson, Mr W. J. Anderson, M.B.E.,
Mr Gordon Hunter, the *Daily Record*, the *Daily Mail*, USGS
Space Frontiers and the Royal Commission on the Ancient
and Historical Monuments of Scotland.

A. M.

Contents

Illustrations

1. The Rudiments of Criticism

When we were boys at the Manse the path from our back gate to Kilblaan was a complicated one.

At first it followed a tree-screened cart-track, rutted by rain water, which curved like a boomerang down to the glebe. Then, approaching the river-bank, it darted off sideways to make use of the 'shooters' ' bridge over the Con. On the opposite bank it plunged improbably into a bramble thicket frilled by primroses, emerging at last beside a hillburn spanned by a 'shoogly' plank. Farther on it climbed a short, steep brae, where purple irises spilled out above a disused lime-kiln. Finally, it made contact with another cart-track leading straight to the farmhouse.

The bridge, hand-railed on one side only, and the plank, less than two feet wide, were always described to us as potential hazards by our anxious mother. But we traversed the path almost daily, because at the end of our journey was Hugh McEachran, our father's kirk treasurer: bachelor Hugh, with his bushy red beard, his carpenter's shop littered with tools and aromatic wood shavings, his heavy Clydesdale horses and sharp-horned Ayrshire cattle and, above all, his enthralling, oath-encrusted stories.

Hugh was an old man when we knew him, with an old man's privileged position as 'the gaffer'. The hard work on the farm was done by his sister Flora and middle-aged bachelor nephew, Archie, while he himself pottered about the steading repairing harness, manufacturing new spokes for damaged cart-wheels, sharpening knives and adzes on a whirling, foot-powered grindstone and, most of all to his taste, attending to and conversing with visitors like us.

At least once a week we were accompanied on our journey to Kilblaan by our father, the Padre, who was not only minister of the parish of Southend at the Mull of Kintyre, but also Hugh's dearest friend.

Hugh's behaviour and attitude to life interested and puzzled us.

He was an elder, a regular churchgoer and a meticulous curator of the pennies and ha'pennies that went into the plate each Sunday, a man whose word was reputed never to have been broken and who did nobody a bad turn if he could help it. His instinct was always to succour people in distress, though he found it difficult to express deep emotion: the only way he could do this was to make himself available at the threshold of a crisis.

During World War II my brother Archie died of wounds following the battle of Gerbini in Sicily. After the Anchor Line's *Britannia* was sunk by an enemy raider, my brother Willie's life-boat remained missing in the South Atlantic for twenty-one days. My brother Kenneth, his reconnaissance Hurricane shot down by the Japanese, was 'lost' for a week in the jungle beyond the Chindwin. On each occasion, while the Padre and my mother – with sister Rona, youngest brother John and Maimie the maid – suffered the deadly news, Hugh was constantly in or around the Manse. When Archie's death was officially announced in a War Office telegram, brought to the Manse by a weeping, trembling postmistress, Hugh was there and remained by my father's side for a long time, holding his hand. When Willie and Kenneth were finally reported safe he rejoiced with my parents, broad 'hechs-hechs' issuing from his beard as preface to the words: 'I tellt ye! I tellt ye they'd be a' richt!'

Hugh was known as a deeply religious man, and he himself would have been surprised if anyone had thought of him as less than Christian. And yet it occurred to us many a time that the flow of his compassion was sometimes interruped when he dealt with people and animals he considered recalcitrant or sinful.

One day my father brought him the news that a member of a well-known local family, for centuries at odds with the McEachrans, had died of influenza. Hugh's reaction astonished us: 'Ach, him! I never kent any o' that lot tae be killed in battle or droont at sea!'

Another day I became distressed by the sorry condition of one of his heifers, which for some time had been refusing to eat and was now slumped disconsolately in its stall. Hugh came down the byre carrying a basket filled with turnips. He emptied them into a trough in front of the sick beast and, in an entirely unsympathetic voice, addressed it thus: 'Bloody wee rascal! Ye'll eat them afore they'll eat ye!' Strangely enough the heifer did eat the turnips and eventually recovered.

Sometimes his horses and cattle sustained open wounds. This was generally the result of their brushing against barbed wire fences or, at a time before the de-horning of Ayrshire cattle became fashionable, of encounters with other head-slashing beasts. Hugh's remedy was always a gout of hot Archangel tar, slapped on with a flat stick apparently without regard to the pain caused to the animal. But we noticed it nearly always brought about a cure.

Fifty years ago long-horned Ayrshire bulls were dangerous animals, especially when they grew older and more short-tempered. (Years later Hugh's nephew was gored to death by one of them.) In their second or third year of duty rings were put in their noses, so that a chain could be attached: a heavy chain which, trailing on the ground, not only hampered their movements in the open fields but could also be secured with a long-handled hay-fork when it became necessary to bring them into the byre.

Archie, Willie and I once witnessed Hugh's method of ringing a bull. First of all he put a long, slim poker into the kitchen fire, so that gradually it would become red hot. Next, with his nephew's help, he turned the bull in its stall and, with ropes, secured it to ring-bolts on either side so that its head hung stiffly over the grip. Then he sent his nephew for a pot of Archangel tar, while he himself went to the kitchen for the poker. As he advanced down the byre, poker stem glowing and sparking, I suddenly realized what was going to happen. Swiftly and without hesitation he plunged the poker through the cartilege inside the bull's nose. His nephew splashed the smoking hole with tar. Hugh himself, discarding the poker, drew the ring from his pocket, opened it, thrust one end through the hole made by the poker and finally snapped it shut.

To this day I can see and hear and smell the operation. I can still feel sick – almost as sick as I felt when the poker burned through flesh and the bull sagged and staggered in its ropes.

But there was another less traumatic day when something happened to Hugh himself which caused us joyful giggles.

As was not unusual on farms in Kintyre, fifty or sixty years ago, the threshing mill, the turnip slicer and various other machines in the barn were driven by water power. Behind Kilblaan was a small dam constantly replenished by a burn which tumbled and twisted down from the hills. When Hugh decided on threshing or slicing he stood on a wooden plank above the dam's outlet to the water-wheel and opened the sluice by means of a rusty crank-handle.

On this warm and sunny afternoon he climbed on to the plank and, puffing and blowing through his beard, began tugging at the crank. Suddenly his foot slipped. He teetered, puffing more than ever, before plunging bodily into the brown water. We rushed to the dam-side, thoughts swirling in our minds concerning a rescue by heroic schoolboys. But the dam was only a few feet deep, and in a moment Hugh emerged unscathed, spouting water like a whale, his scanty hair dripping with slime and water-lily leaves.

His immediate reaction was unexpected. In his waistcoat pocket, secured by a chain with a fob to it, he kept a silver watch that had belonged to his father, a fat hunter-type at least three inches in diameter. It was his dearest possession. Now, as he erupted from the deep, like Poseidon, he took no thought of his own condition. He whipped out the watch, surveyed it, held it against his ear and then announced to us with a triumphant smile: 'She's gaun, boys! She's still gaun!'

In spite of all the contradictions in his character, in spite of an Old Testament severity in some areas of conduct, Hugh had a faith which was the envy of us all. As he lay on his death-bed my father sat by him.

'I can see, Hugh,' said the Padre, 'that you're not afraid to die.'

'Feart, minister?' said Hugh, whispering his surprise. 'Why should I be feart?'

The McEachrans are of old Kintyre stock. Their name comes from the Gaelic, meaning 'sons of the horsemen'. It keeps recurring in old deeds and titles dating back to the sixteenth century; it is probable that the family is descended from the *Epidii*, the Celtic tribe which prompted Ptolemy, in the second century AD, to call Kintyre *Epidion Akron*, the land of the horsemen.

Cnoc Araich, a green hill beetle-browed with whins, is situated immediately behind the Manse on High Machrimore Farm, confronting Kilblaan across the valley of the Con. On its flat summit, covering about six acres, there can be seen the remains of a settlement dating from about 600 BC to 400 AD. With the Royal Commission on the Ancient and Historical Monuments of Scotland I share a theory about this *dun*. On account of its size, may it not have been the headquarters (or principal village) of the *Epidii*?

Listening, as a boy, to the Padre and Hugh discussing Cnoc Araich, I had an impression of Southend as a place in which roots go very deep; even then I think my ambition was to continue nurturing my roots in the same warm and fertile soil.

But the stories about old Southend which Hugh used to tell – stories to which we listened with the quiet concentration gifted only to children – were not only concerned with the question of family roots; they were also powerfully stimulating to the imagination. It may be that as I listened to them the idea was born that one day I, too, would become a storyteller. And possibly it was Hugh's own character, so difficult to analyse, that caused me to become permanently interested in people, the raw material out of which a storyteller constructs his products.

Later on I found that my father and mother – and Maimie, the maid – were equally fascinating characters; but at the age of nine or ten I viewed my parents and Maimie not as ordinary human beings but simply as rock-like symbols of security and authority, untrammelled by weakness, like the Holy Trinity.

Hugh's stories were much to our taste. Concerning wreckers, smugglers, poachers and other enemies of an organized society, they provided source material for many plays enacted by my brothers and myself in the Manse back yard.

The main character in one of Hugh's most acceptable stories was Black Angus MacNacht. It is said that he lived in the late sixteenth century in Gartvaigh, a farm which lies over the hill immediately behind Achnamara. According to Hugh he was a powerful man with long black hair and whiskers and a voice that could be heard 'a bloody mile away'. ('Bloody' was Hugh's favourite adjective. We were assured by the Padre that, unlike us young sophisticates, he had no idea it was a swear word.)

In his public image Black Angus was a diligent farmer, a responsible member of the community, regular in his attendance at religious services. But behind this appearance of respectability there lurked a secret: a secret making nonsense of the name MacNacht, which comes from a Pictish word meaning 'pure'. He was the leader of a wrecking gang.

Across the bay from my study window I can see the Rock of Dunaverty, a turf-coated lump of Old Red Sandstone thirty metres tall. On its northern flank there used to stand a Clan Donald Castle, the meagre ruins of which can still be discovered among the grass and the nettles. In the sixteenth century, when Black Angus prowled in the night, it must have been an imposing fortress, though in winter, when bad weather dampened the ardour of the battling clans and fighting MacDonalds went home to their wives and children in Antrim and Islay, it was often left untenanted. At such times its empty western battlements provided the ideal site for a peat-fired brazier.

As Hugh carefully explained to us, a beacon often burned on the island of Sanda, two miles south-east of Dunaverty across the Sound, dutifully lit by the member of Clan Donald currently holding the island in feu. Vessels entering the North Channel from the north or west, rounding the Mull of

Kintyre on their way into the Clyde, kept this light on their starboard bow and found a safe passage between Sanda and the mainland. But on a dark night, with showers of hail sweeping down from the hills, the master of a small ship hugging the sheltered coast of the Mull might become confused and, seeing a light on Dunaverty, believe it to be the one on Sanda. Too late he would discover he was heading not for the Sound but for the black rocks of the Gearraidh Dubh. (They thrust long, ugly fingers into the sea less than fifty metres from our front door.)

And on the Gearraidh Dubh Black Angus and his gang would be waiting. When survivors struggled ashore throats would be slit and bodies hurled back into the sea. The vessel would be boarded and the cargoes of cloth and rum and timber carried stealthily away to secluded barns and caves.

The people of the parish knew the truth but were afraid to reveal it to the representatives of law and order, in those days the local chieftains of Clan Donald. Black Angus and his henchmen had spread the word that informers would be dealt with, by maiming or even death.

At this point in the story Hugh would pause, half-hidden eyes glinting at us from behind stiff red lashes. 'But bad men,' he would tell us, while the Padre nodded grave confirmation, 'bad men aye come tae a bad end.'

We waited. We needed proof. We wanted proof.

'One wild nicht,' said Hugh, at last, 'the wreckers put a licht on Dunaverty. After a while they saw a boat makin' for the Gearraidh Dubh. She was high at prow an' stern, no' like the ordinary cargo vessels sailin' between Antrim and the Clyde. But they werena worried aboot that. They'd never yet seen a boat that hadna somethin' valuable in her. So they rushed doon tae the shore, ready for action.

'The boat cam' closer, veered a bit tae the eastward, then struck – no' on the black rocks but on the soft sand o' Dunaverty Bay. This wasna what usually happened, but still the wreckers had nae inklin' o' danger. They dashed intae the surf, wi' their clubs an' knives, an' climbed aboard.

'At first they could see naebody. Then oot o' the hatches cam' a hale airmy o' men, armed wi' swords an' shields.

Black Angus an' his gang were cut doon an' killed an' fed tae
the fishes.'

Archie and Willie and I let out breaths of excitement and
satisfaction. 'But who were the armed men in the boat?' I
asked.

'A Clan Donald chieftain an' his sodgers. Frae Islay.
Comin' tae garrison Dunaverty Castle. Roondin' the Mull
they were deceived by the licht on Dunaverty, but then, as
they neared the shore, they jaloused what was gaun on an'
steered for the sand. Their galley was refloated next day, at
high tide. But' – and here Hugh chuckled – 'Black Angus
didna float again.'

Is this a true story? I believe it may contain some truth. In
the parish records I find there were MacNachts in Gartvaigh
from 1505 until early in the seventeenth century and that the
common family name was Angus. But I imagine that in the
telling, over the centuries, it has acquired dramatic and
moralistic qualities geared more to fiction than to fact.

The violence in it, and the apparent callousness of the
narrator, may be compared with some offerings by today's
cinema and television. Had it a bad effect on our tender
minds? I shivered when I heard it, but at the same time a
thought was planted in my ethical garden. 'Bad men aye
come tae a bad end.' In modern films and plays this proposition is sometimes overlooked and violence presented simply
for the sake of violence, with evil remaining unpunished. Is
this the inartistic factor which renders the portrayal of violence dangerous to young viewers? Maybe so. In real life
violence is always punished, either physically or spiritually.
Has there ever existed an evil man who was happy?

Archie, Willie and I found ourselves in a privileged position.

We listened to Hugh's horrific stories and witnessed the
life on his farm, where procreation, birth, savagery and
death were regarded in a realistic and unsensational way. We
grew up with few illusions about the natural world, thus
avoiding the traumatic experiences of some adolescents
brought up to believe in fairies and happy endings and animals acting and talking like human beings.

We were supplied with no pocket money. The Padre, living in a Manse with eleven rooms on an annual stipend of about £300, had none to offer. And Hugh, in those days of neglected agriculture, had no surplus cash to waste on children. For the odd half-crown to buy ice-cream and Sharpe's 'Super Kreme Toffee' we had to depend on our own wits: for example, on the sale to a scrap merchant of lead bullets surreptitiously dug out of the sand behind the Territorial Army target on Brunerican shore and to a dealer in Campbeltown of stamps collected from people in the parish with relatives abroad. This, I believe was good for us. When, later on, we had to fend for ourselves in a society with about 2 500 000 unemployed (and no 'social security') we were well equipped to endure and eventually overcome bouts of poverty. And when the Welfare State did come – blessed though it was – we had enough independence of spirit to avoid its enervating influence. Though Hugh and the Padre had no money to give they presented us with something far more valuable: the idea that the source of real happiness is obedience to the ten commandments and the giving of love and consideration to other people.

I, for one, have broken many commandments. Hate has burgeoned in my heart for a few of my neighbours. The desire to commit crude violence has often invaded me like a sickness. Each time the experience has made me miserable; and my conviction has grown stronger that to follow the realistic Christianity advocated by Hugh and the Padre is the only way to a good life.

Sometimes, as I grow older, I imagine I have found this good life. More often I recognize how sadly I have missed the way.

While ethical principles were being received and vaguely understood by my brothers and myself, other influences were at work. I was listening to Hugh's stories about Southend, to my father's about his native North Uist, to my mother's about her younger days in Appin and to Maimie's renderings of old-fashioned narrative poetry (like *Horatius* and *Barbara Freitchie*) and her whispered ghost tales of

Perthshire. An excitement occurred inside me, focusing into an ambition to tell stories of my own, in words of my own choosing. Even then the vanity of a writer was apparent: I dreamt of the day when my name would appear in a magazine or – joy of joys – on the cover of a book.

But I acknowledged to myself a lack of confidence in my tools. It was hard to find words and phrases that would, without ambiguity, convey my meaning. When I wrote something down it appeared childish to me. I failed to understand that I *was* a child.

My mother kept a copy of my first 'poem'. When she died in 1963 a small cardboard box was found in the drawer of her dressing-table. It contained her few private treasures, and the 'poem' was one of them.

> Willie MacVicar, the boy of the day,
> Has dogs and dollies and teddy-bears.
> He has a sad and unfortunate habit
> Of kicking them when he is crabbit.

I remember being ashamed of having to use the word 'crabbit', which is Scots for 'bad-tempered'; but there was no other way – or so it seemed to me – that I could procure a rhyme for 'habit'. (I wasn't completely satisfied with 'bears' as a proper rhyme for 'day', but with a writer's unflinching optimism I hoped it might get by.) In those days Scots (or Gaelic) words were considered crude, the Stone Age tools of the uneducated. Magisterial influence directed my sights on the 'correct' English of the school 'readers'. *Chambers's Radical Reading*, for example, contained excerpts from the works of H. B. Stowe, H. S. Pemberton, Christina Rosetti and others.

Today the scene in Scotland has changed. When I was young only roadmen, farm-labourers and elderly waitresses were called Jamie and Jock and Maggie. Now it is the height of fashion to own such names, and the Cyrils, the Georges and the Daphnes are reserved for another stratum of 'society'. Sir Walter Scott was then the exemplar of good writing. When we went to Campbeltown Grammar School from Southend in 1920, one of the first books we were told to buy was *Scott's Narrative Poetry* published by Nelson. At that time Burns's Tam O'Shanter was ignored and its author described condescendingly as 'the ploughboy poet'. Now poor old Sir Walter is no longer considered a genius in the use of English (though even the BBC admits that his plots are still the greatest) and Burns, in spite of using the word 'crabbit' many times, is universally admired. Indeed, the Edinburgh 'literati' would claim that the late C. M. Grieve is the proper example for a young writer, even though as Hugh McDiarmid, Grieve often wrote in Lallans, an invented Scots language which might be described as dead had it ever been alive.

For the most part, fashion in writing is created by the political and economic climate of the age, and, to a large extent by the critics. It is something which must be taken into account if a writer wishes to sell his work and thus communicate with as many of his fellow human beings as possible, but any author or poet worth his salt will ignore fashion if he believes it to be an inhibiting factor. On mature consideration I'm glad I called Willie 'crabbit'.

But at the age of twelve, brain-washed by an 'English' orientated education, I knew little about Scottish history or culture. (Indeed, my ignorance in this area remained almost total until after I went to grammar school and my father advised me to read *Tales of a Grandfather*.) I had a vague notion that I wanted to write about the people of Southend and their situation, but immediately after World War I nobody seemed to be interested in the ordinary folk of Southend. I felt I ought to be aiming higher – at, for example, the exciting and, at the time, highly popular stories about Bulldog Drummond. The fact that I knew nothing about the English society in which Bulldog Drummond moved and had his Fascist being worried me a lot less than it should have.

My only available target, therefore, seemed to be the enormous market for short stories which existed in the 1920s. In London, that is.

A beginning writer today, desperately seeking a home for his work, may well gasp with envy when confronted by the following (alphabetical) list of magazines willing and eager to buy short stories in 1923: *The Blue Magazine, Cassell's Magazine, Corner Magazine, The Happy Mag, The Home Magazine, Hutchinson's Magazine, Hutchinson's Adventure Story Magazine, London Magazine, Mystery Story Magazine, Nash's Magazine, New Magazine, The Novel Magazine, Pan, Pearson's Magazine, Premier Magazine, The Red Magazine, Romance, The Smart Set, Sovereign Magazine, The Storyteller, The Strand Magazine, Twenty Story Magazine, Violet Magazine, The Windsor Magazine, The Yellow Magazine.*

On being approached by a youth with Kintyre heather in his ears, the editor of *The Green Magazine* – a rose in the flourishing chaplet of the Amalgamated Press – detailed his requirements thus: '(a) strong adventure stories, with clearly drawn characters; (b) light, humorous stories, ingenious but not too involved, with witty dialogue; (c) well-constructed "crook" stories, with novel but not sensational situations; (d) sporting stories if off conventional lines and with human interest; (e) a few nature stories by authors who know their subject, preferably of such animals as lions, bears, etc., and stories of any type that will appeal to men and women alike. Length, about five thousand words.'

My knowledge of adventure was limited to poaching salmon in the burn which meandered through the Manse glebeland and to launching homemade rafts in the shallow rapids below the Minister's Lynn. I suspected that a London editor might scoff at such tame pursuits. English humour and dialogue considered witty by an Englishman was, I feared, beyond my capability. I knew nothing about 'crooks' – that is, about the jewel thieves, con men and train robbers so often described in the magazine stories I so avidly read. I had never encountered a lion or a bear – or even, let it be said, a fox – except in print. On the other hand, I felt that I might be able to write a sporting story, 'off conventional lines and with human interest'. After all, I played football, cricket and golf and had won a few junior races at the Highland Games.

The editor of *London Magazine* was more intimidating. 'The short story that counts,' he wrote, 'is that which deals with life *as it is*: the characters should not be merely creatures of the author's imagination, but living, breathing actors in the story he has to tell. The soul-storms arising from love, jealousy, passion – all these things make stories if logically and not too theatrically treated. They may be placed in Mayfair or Bermondsey, but if the psychology be true they are certain of their following. Either a story is written because it *had* to be written, or it is merely part of the day's work of the author.'

Today, contemplating this vision of splendour, I take a deep breath – and then do a double take. As a twelve-year-old I was discouraged. I reckoned I had not yet experienced a 'soul-storm'. And 'life *as it is*', apparently to be found only in Mayfair or Bermondsey, was a far cry from the hills and salt-sprayed beaches of Southend.

But it occurred to me that if I failed to reach those high sierras of the fictional art I might still have a chance with the hundreds of weekly and juvenile publications which also bought short stories – publications ranging from *Answers, Tit-bits, John o'London's Weekly, Home Chat* and *Woman's Pictorial* to *The Boy's Own Paper, Captain* and *Chums*.

In Scotland I could discover only two magazines which published short stories: *Blackwood's* and *Chambers's Journal*. By the high-powered and somewhat patronising market guides they were described as 'literary', for no other reason, it seemed to me, than that they paid only a guinea a thousand words, whereas London editors offered two guineas a thousand even to unknown writers.

So there I was, a country boy seduced by artificiality, with an urge to write. Though I discussed the subject with no one – especially not with my parents, who were eager that I should become a minister of the Kirk – I felt that I *could* write. The trouble was that I had no confidence that what I wrote could be exchanged for editorial money. Already what has been described as 'author's schizophrenia' was beginning to haunt me. I wanted to be a good writer. I also wanted to be rich.

Today, more than fifty years on, I am bothered with the same affliction.

One evening my brothers and I visited Kilblaan and found that a stranger – a distant relative of the McEachrans – had come to recuperate there after an illness. He was a young man, in his twenties, the son of a former schoolmaster in Southend. As a child of ten, on the Hebridean island of Coll, he had been watching builders at work, when a granite 'skelf', one of a shower sent up by a careless stone-mason's hammer and chisel, had lodged in one eye. Soon afterwards he had become totally blind.

It was our first encounter with a blind person. We were disturbed by the pale, thin face into which suffering had been cut as if by a knife, and by the dark glasses which did not completely hide wrinkled and empty eye-sockets. We felt fear and resentment: fear of the unknown, resentment of an ugliness which had invaded our comfortable small paradise.

His name was James MacTaggart. With astonishment we discovered he was not only an accomplished musician but also, through the medium of Braille, a student of English literature. From the Manse piano and the church organ he produced thrilling sounds; he sang Scots and Irish songs in a lusty baritone at odds with his fragile looks. He composed music of his own and married it to verses he himself had written. In addition he played chess on a special board constructed by a friend. The pieces were pegged into small holes, and as the game went on his fingers kept passing over the chessmen so that their relative positions might remain in his mind's eye.

At first we were shy of him, but as the months – and years – of his convalescence went by, and he became an accepted member of the community, I, for one, found his company fascinating. He was an artist, I was a lumpish schoolboy, tutored to some extent in the physical and religious aspects of life but eager to learn about literature and music and what Neil Munro used to call 'the strange cantrips of the human heart'. James was willing to teach me all he knew.

He taught me chess, demonstrating on his board some classic openings used by the masters. I enjoyed the game well enough but was never able to beat him, except when he arranged that I should. I think his blindness gave him a power of concentration beyond my scope.

He presented me with a book called *The Rudiments of Criticism*, which dealt with a concept new to me: the power of words to create music when read aloud. I began to be aware of clashing consonents and the ugly effect of too many similar vowel sounds crowded together. It also indicated how word sounds could evoke a scene, a situation, an emotion. James and I talked about *A Musical Instrument*, by Elizabeth Barrett Browning, and agreed that it illustrated both ideas.

> What was he doing, the great god Pan
> > Down in the reeds by the river?
> Spreading ruin and scattering ban,
> Splashing and paddling with hoofs of a goat,
> And breaking the golden lilies afloat
> > With the dragon-fly on the river.
>
> Yet half a beast is the great god Pan,
> > To laugh as he sits by the river,
> Making a poet out of a man:
> The true gods sigh for the cost and pain, –
> For the reed which grows nevermore again
> > As a reed with the reeds in the river.

Many years later, when I began to write for radio, this lesson remained with me; and Scots actors like the late Bryden Murdoch, Jameson Clark and Madeleine Christie have told me they usually found my writing easy to speak. My slightly sardonic friend, Archie P. Lee, a BBC producer now retired, once paid me a back-handed compliment: 'Your scripts, Angus, often sound a lot better than they read.'

As we talked about writing, James surprised me by his ability to 'see' words on the printed page. 'Grey', he said, 'always suggests to me something dark and sinister. "Gray" is light coloured, almost sparkling.' Ever since then I have used the different spellings according to James's ideas.

But James had more wisdom to impart.

His own stories and verses, generally based on the folk lore of Kintyre, had a vigorous life which, though it might not find favour in a sophisticated London market, I admired and resolved to cultivate, if I could. His thin, strong fingers danced across the keys of a piano with the same vigour; and in those days, when the 'wireless' was only an intriguing toy, when television was unknown and few people had cars to convey them the ten miles to a cinema in Campbeltown, he was much in demand at ceilidhs in the Manse and at the local farms.

Towards the end of his stay in Southend, when I was about sixteen, he instituted a singing class in the church hall, which was attended by almost every young person in the parish. He conducted it for love, not for money. In those post-war days of agricultural hardship, before marketing-boards were created and when the idea of subsidies was a mere twinkle in the eye of an astute Farmers' Union secretary, the spending of money on an artistic pursuit would have been considered 'daft' by country folk. Not only 'daft' but criminal. But – 'There's nobody who can't sing,' James told us with gusto. 'When you feel happy you want to sing. I'll teach you how.'

So we all sang, in our various fashions, and though it soon became apparent that in certain individual cases our teacher's optimism outpaced reality, it was arranged that before dispersing for the summer the class should give a 'grand' concert in the Territorial Hall, a more commodious and important venue than the church hall.

Parents, aunts, uncles and cousins were thrilled to anticipate the appearance of relatives on the platform. The show, therefore, was a 'sell out'. Under hissing pressure lamps and surrounded by an aroma of paraffin from heaters placed in handy corners, the audience settled back on wooden benches to enjoy it.

A young piper opened the programme. He was Ronald MacCallum, one of a family of dancers and musicians famous in Kintyre and, indeed, throughout Scotland and the Commonwealth. In later years he became a Scottish champion and piper in residence to the Duke of Argyll at Inveraray Castle.

Then, one after another, in various states of alarm and euphoria, we trooped on stage to 'do our thing'. Some of us were good singers: for example the McKerral boys from Brunerican and their small sister, Jean. They were the show-stoppers – and continued to be show-stoppers at many a festival and concert in years to come. The rest of us filled in as best as we could.

One tall, usually happy girl gave a rendering of *Whistle and I'll come tae ye, my lad*. Swaying nervously from side to side, her note rising ever higher to the edge of hysteria, she had all the young blades in the audience loudly obeying her instructions before she was done.

Another girl, who had a lovely alto voice, took stage fright halfway through her piece and ran, weeping, from the platform.

I sang a ballad called *The Wee Toon Clerk* which, to everyone's dismay, I still sing when fortified by a dram or two. As I began the second verse I caught the eye of Mrs Morton, my former teacher in Southend Public School. She was shaking with suppressed laughter, not at the words of the song but at me. In a blur of embarrassment I, too, started to laugh and retired from the scene pursued by cat-calls from unsympathetic school friends.

James also was unsympathetic. 'Why should you be embarrassed? Singing is as natural as breathing. Express yourself. Enjoy yourself. And if people scoff and won't listen, why worry! You're growing up within yourself.'

At the time I understood only vaguely what he meant.

About James there was a lust for living that was contagious. But, unlike that of the great god Pan, it was a lust tempered by gentleness and romance. On winter evenings at Brunerican he and Jean McKerral took turns to play accompaniments on the piano, while the McKerral brothers sang and their father and I listened. The little girl who had been my partner at a dancing class years before was now fifteen, and as James sang his songs of love I would catch her eye and find that she was aware of me, too.

There was stirrings in my blood. I was being offered fabulous delights, both spiritual and physical. Had I the courage to accept them?

One night I was at Kilblaan, listening to James, with old Hugh and his nephew Archie, talking about the thatchers and potato gatherers who used to cross the North Channel from Ireland to work on the Southend farms, bringing their songs and stories with them. Near midnight I said goodnight to the McEachrans and went out through the front porch into a wall of darkness. I had no torch, and the thought of the complicated path to the Manse gave me a moment of uneasiness.

'I'll see you across the bridge,' said James, behind me.

'I wish you would,' I said. Then, with sudden anxiety: 'But it's so dark! Will you manage back on your own?'

James laughed, and as he laughed I remembered. 'Sorry,' I said.

'I'm not sorry,' he told me, 'so why should you be. Come on.'

2. Ink in My Veins

When James MacTaggart left Kilblaan, for me a mite of magic was withdrawn. The ideal of writing for the sake of good writing began to blur. Being without material capital of any kind, I was being pressed towards the conclusion that writing for money rather than for artistic reasons should be my aim. I had little of the true poet's disregard for moral and physical comfort. In a situation of low wages and high unemployment I wanted to achieve financial independence.

It may seem ironical that after half a century of writing for a living, putting by each year a little silver in my sporran, I have not as yet achieved this independence. But I have achieved something else: I can live with my writing and not be ashamed of it.

James himself had to face hard facts. He married his Maid Marian and took a job in Helensburgh as a music teacher. He also became a church organist, training his choir with the same optimism and enthusiasm he had shown in Southend. And there was no namby-pampy holiness about his organ playing. When the mood of the music demanded it, the stone pillars and the stained-glass windows reverberated, echoing its power.

James and his wife now live in retirement in Campbeltown. In his mid-seventies, he still strides through the streets, fearing nothing, occasionally coming to grief against an unexpected pile of pavement rubble, but in the main giving the impression that his blindness is only a minor inconvenience. When someone greets him he recognizes the voice at once.

For more than twenty years – during World War II and for a time afterwards, while he worked in Helensburgh – I lost touch with him. One day, by a thousand to one chance, I encountered him in a Glasgow street.

'Hullo, James. How's the health?'

The reply came without the slightest hesitation. 'Angus! Great to see you again – in Glasgow of all places!'

(He always 'sees' old friends and acquaintances.)

His daughter is a doctor. His elder son, after a spell as editor of the *Campbeltown Courier*, now works with the Canadian government. His second son is a pilot instructor with the RAF. James's bravery – and that of his Maid Marian in becoming the wife of a blind man – were transmitted to them all.

For a time Dr Mary practised medicine in Ghana, though her fair skin and auburn hair made it fairly certain that the hot climate would prove a continual burden. While editor of the *Courier* Victor's outspoken reporting delighted the local community. Like his father, recovering quickly after stumbling over an unaccustomed obstacle, he would attack snobbery in one issue and then, with undiminished enthusiasm, tilt against ignorance in the next. Ian flies with nervous and unskilled pilots and thinks nothing of the danger.

My admiration for James is based partly on his artistic accomplishments but mainly, I think, on his courage. It has nothing bombastic about it and produces no specific incidents which a public relations officer could work up into newspaper headlines. It is natural, continuing and enduring, woven into the fabric of his life.

James has been a constant inspiration as far as I, an ordinary person and an ordinary writer, am concerned. He and people like him are seldom identified by the media. Newspapers, television and radio prefer to deal with characters whose lives exemplify extreme righteousness or extreme sinfulness. For them, stories concerning the discipline and courage shown day after day and year after year by ordinary folk are not dramatic enough. To use a journalistic phrase, they have 'less impact'. But such stories – and James's story in particular – appeal to me. They comfort me when I take a sour view of humanity, and strengthen me when I despair of my own courage and endurance.

It is said that God – whosoever or whatsoever He may be – rejoices in great saints and also in great sinners who come to repentance. But few of us are saints, either great or small, and fewer still are flagrant sinners who repent. Does God not also rejoice over his numerous 'middlemen', unnoticed and unsung though they appear to be? I must say I wouldn't have much faith in Him if He didn't.

I had – and still have – a stammer, a minor infirmity compared with James's blindness. But at times it can be traumatic, especially for a writer, who is occasionally compelled in the course of business to communicate with his fellows by word of mouth. Quite often, while waiting in sweaty anxiety for a television camera to blink red, or a desk-bulb in a radio studio to flash me cruelly into action, or for a chairman to end an apparently endless speech of introduction, I have thought of James, in darkness and doubt, striding with relentless courage into danger. And the thought has always helped me.

When publishers and editors regret and reject, when critics dismiss months of hard work in two or three careless lines, when bankers print DR against a monthly statement, at such times I also think of James. He has to bear similar human disappointments. But he is blind, and I am not. And, forgetting my stammer, I thank God for the mercy of sight and get on with the business of restoring my material situation.

I spent six years as a pupil at Campbeltown Grammar School. During this time, from 1920 until 1926, my stammer was no great inconvenience – to me, at any rate. Obviously it had an effect on some teachers, because, usually after a few short, shattering experiments, they were inclined to dispense with my contributions during question and answer sessions. This suited me admirably and caused me to become an envied personality among my classmates. It also resulted in careless home-work and an increasing indulgence in the idleness which lies at the root of my nature.

On the whole my schooldays in Campbeltown were happy. Living in 'digs' from Monday to Friday, ten miles out of range of parental eyes (and of Maimie's hard knuckles) and supervised only by a kind and indulgent landlady, I enjoyed considerable freedom. On clear nights in spring and autumn my mates and I would play football or cricket on a weird pitch halfway up a mountain, or fish from the pier or swan around the harbour in a rowing boat belonging to Big Allan MacDougall's father. On winter nights we would roam the streets in gangs, sometimes enacting cowboy and Indian dramas, howling and cat-calling up and down dark closes, sometimes chasing willing girls, only to discover when we caught them that we had no precise idea what to do with them. (Lambs leaping and running in the fields in spring have the same problem.)

Away from the influence of the Manse, I am afraid that for me ethical questions tended to receive hazy answers. At one stage, in our first year, Davie Watson and I carried out a scheme which may rank in iniquity, if not in scope, with some of the big business operations which have caused scandals in modern times.

One of our teachers – for history and geography – was Kate Stalker, an elderly maiden lady of forthright speech and manner, with piled-up grey hair and heavy spectacles. Boys and girls who came from junior schools in the country were popular with her, because, as she kept on declaring, they were better educated and more polite than the children of the town. As Watson's home was twelve miles north of Campbeltown and mine was in Southend we were among her favourites.

At the beginning of the year, as she noted our names, I remember how one town girl revealed, timidly, that her name was Valerie Joy. An insulting sound came from Kate's hooked nose. 'Valerie Joy?' she exclaimed. 'I know your mother and your granny, Mary and Jeannie. Less would do you!'

One day she lectured us about poor children of the past, children forced to work in the pits, on the farms, as chimney-sweepers' assistants. A harrowing recital which caused Valerie Joy to burst into tears. 'Huh!' said Kate. 'Tears are no good. The reformers may have cried a little, but they were also practical, and so must you be! There are still many poor and neglected children in the big cities, and it is up to you, pampered and privileged creatures that you are, to do something for them. I want some volunteers to go around the town and collect money for the National Society for the Prevention of Cruelty to Children.'

A wary hush fell upon the class. Young as we were, experience had taught us that volunteering for anything was liable to be a mug's game, a waste of time that could be spent in more pleasurable pursuits. In any case, volunteering at the behest of a teacher was a sure way to earn the title of 'sook'. ('Sucking up' was an expression which, I believe, originated in World War I and may have come, like many another linguistic gem, from America. Until World War II it applied to other ranks and employees who toadied to officers and employers. Nowadays officers and employers 'suck up' to other ranks and employees.)

In the end, faced by continuing silence, Kate had to use conscription. She pointed to and named two 'townies' and, with a sniff of disgust for our lack of social conscience, handed them collecting tins and a bundle of NSPCC literature.

Later in the day, however, when we found time to discuss it, Watson and I came to the conclusion that there might, after all, be some fun in a collecting round. I don't think the idea of financial profit had yet occurred to us. We looked forward to spending happy hours importuning the parents of some of our classmates and being rewarded with the occasional apple or slice of tasty cake. It would also provide a noble excuse if critical comments were made about our homework. Privately, therefore, and letting nobody else know, we spoke to Kate and told her we wished to help her with the collecting job.

She was delighted. We couldn't have collecting tins, she explained, because she'd been allocated only two, and these had been given to the conscripts. But would we take some leaflets to show possible subscribers?

'Yes, ma'am,' we said, with self-righteous smirks.

During the next two evenings we enjoyed ourselves. It was

January. The weather was cold and wet and we took pride in looking bedraggled as we stood on doorsteps and proferred leaflets. We collected sweets in satisfying quantities – also, to our surprise, what seemed to us enormous sums of money for the NSPCC. A ten-shilling note offered by a solicitor's wife made us blink with astonishment.

The principal reason for our success may have been that our respective parents, though living in the country, were well known and respected in the town. It is possible, too, that our soaked and shivering appearance, part natural, part assumed, may have touched the hearts of kindly folk.

At the end of the second night we discovered that in the tea-caddy provided by Watson's landlady we had just over £12. In 1921 this was sensational, the equivalent of about £100 today. As we counted it up at my digs we looked into each other's eyes and saw there the dawn of corruption.

We argued it out in what we both considered was a sensible and logical way. Kate would be glad to get as much as £10. So would the children who suffered cruelty. If we kept a pound each for ourselves it would only be just reward for the hard work we had done in adverse weather conditions.

'Our expenses,' said Watson.

'That's it,' I agreed. 'And anyway, people are cruel to *us* at times. We're entitled to something.'

Kate was overjoyed when we handed her the £10, along with a few extra coppers to demonstrate our supreme honesty. The conscripts with the collecting tins had got only about a pound between them. They were dismissed by her as 'useless', while Watson and I were lauded in public as boys of initiative and solid worth.

We kept our secret to ourselves, and everybody – everybody, that is, except perhaps the two conscripts, whose collecting tins were sealed and the contents, therefore, inviolable – appeared to be happy. But ever since then my conscience has troubled me. The pound in my pocket represented a hundred and twenty ice-cream 'sliders', riches beyond dreams. But I felt guilty – and still do, in spite of the widespread modern tolerance of inflated expense accounts.

I don't know about Watson. He became a highly successful chartered accountant.

As we laboured towards our fifth year we found most of our
fun in the Latin class.

Our Latin class would have provided an interesting case-
history for modern educationists, sociologists and psychiat-
rists.

The master was thin and pale, aged about thirty. It was
rumoured that during World War I he had suffered shell-
shock; but his war experiences could have been scarcely
more disturbing than those he endured as a teacher. A
strange smell emanated from his person – or it could have
been from his clothes, which, as a rule, consisted of a folded
cloth muffler instead of a collar and a threadbare grey suit. It
was an acrid smell, the cause of which I have never been able
to diagnose. He appeared to exist in a continual state of
secret anger and frustration. Sometimes, for no apparent
reason, beads of sweat would stand out on his forehead while
he thrust forward a doubled-up tongue and chewed on it
with savage jaws.

This unfortunate man was given the task of dealing with a
mob of children who, given the slightest chance, would
behave like hooligans. He gave us that chance and, being
cruel and sadistic, we considered it sport to make his life
even more of a misery than it already was.

He kept a Lochgelly strap, folded over once, continually in
his right hand. When we boys made rude noises or gestured
defiance he would leap at us, strap flailing, and deliver blow
after blow on the backs of our necks. When the girls misbe-
haved he would control himself with a visibly hurtful effort,
essay a deathshead smile and plead for obedience in a voice
strained almost to breaking-point. If his control slipped, and
he did flick the strap at a girl's arm or hand, we would stamp
our feet and set up a growling chant: 'Ah-h-h, bully! Leave
the girls alone!' At which he would stride away from the
class, lean awkwardly against his desk with his thin, stooped
back towards us, and bite the forefinger of the hand which
held the strap. The chant would swell: 'Bully! Bully!' And at

last, like a desperate animal, he would swing round and throw himself among us, lashing out in all directions.

The blows from his strap didn't worry us. Over the years the skin on the backs of our necks became as tough and insensitive as leather. We also perfected a technique of hunching. This ensured that most of the blows fell upon our shoulders, which, with intelligent forethought, we padded with newspapers.

At the beginning, so indiscriminate were his lashings, that the strap sometimes struck against our heads and ears. This was definitely painful and had to be stopped. We staged a salutary happening, therefore, with Alastair MacMillan in the principal role.

'*Soporiferumque papaver*,' intoned Alastair and continued, with error aforethought, to translate: 'And the blessed poppy went to sleep.'

'Stop, you fool!' cried the master, employing his customary epithet. '*Soporiferumque papaver* means "And the sleep-bringing poppy"!'

'Excuse me, sir,' said Alastair, who was tall, elegant and well-spoken, the son of an exciseman, 'are you not forgetting the words in the Bible: "Whosoever shall say, Thou fool, shall be in danger of hell's fire"?' (As a son of the Manse I had forearmed Alastair with the exact quotation.)

The master's body became taut. He began to chew upon his tongue. His eyes glazed. Then he bared his teeth and lunged savagely at Alastair, who by this time had sat down. Blow succeeded blow until at last, with a hoarse scream, Alastair reared up, staggered forward and finally fell prone against the master's desk.

The girls set up a moaning. Big Allan and Davie Watson and I sprang forward to kneel beside the casualty. The master's face was yellow-white. He stood over us, small strangled sounds bubbling in his throat.

Big Allan said: 'You struck him on the head, sir.'

'A wild blow,' said Davie Watson.

I put an ear to Alastair's chest. I said: 'Is he dead, sir?'

The moaning of the girls became a Hebridean coronach. The master looked terrified. He wrung his hands, which became entangled with the strap. He turned pitifully to May Ollar, a blonde tomboy who sat in front. 'Get water! Get brandy!' he whispered between dry lips.

'Wait!' I said. 'His heart's beating again!'

Following the script, Alastair began to stir. 'My head! My head!' he groaned. (Looking back on it, after a lifetime's experience of writing documentaries for TV and radio, I must admit the script wasn't all that bad, based as it was on an intimate knowledge of the character.)

The girls ceased their moaning, uttering instead glad and hopeful cries.

'It's a miracle!' said Big Allan. 'He's coming round!'

Davie Watson's strong hands helped Alastair to his feet. Ineffectually dabbing, alternately smiling with inane relief and chewing on his tongue, the master attempted to dust his clothes.

Alastair said: 'I want to see the headmaster.'

The master grew even pastier. 'Please, MacMillan, is there any need – '

Watson and I said: 'You nearly killed him, sir!'

'I – I'm sorry. It was an accident.'

'Well,' said Alastair, 'if you'll promise not to hit any of us on the head again. I mean, it's all right on the shoulders, but – '

'Certainly, certainly! I'll put the strap away for good. If there's anything else I can do . . .'

Looking back, I realize what sickening, hypocritical, violent creatures we were. The Latin class had the attraction for us of an unusual adventure, spiced with danger. We gave no consideration to the fact that for the master, probably ill, both physically and mentally, it must have been slow agony. I suppose that nowadays we should have been ideal recruitment fodder for the National Front, which plays upon and encourages the normal sadistic instincts of youth.

After the MacMillan 'happening' the master did not, of course, put his strap away. He continued to deliver blows, though not so often against our heads and ears. We continued to bait him, much to our enjoyment.

One of our classmates was Davie McArthur, who in childhood had contracted polio and, as a result, wore a caliper on one wasted leg. In spite of his infirmity, Davie had a wicked imagination and an IQ higher than the average. Years later, it was no surprise to me when, as headmaster of a junior school, he had several ingenious Scottish plays broadcast on BBC radio. His youthful torture of the Latin master took the form of an intellectual rather than a physical exercise.

In the top of his desk was a small knot-hole, which had been enlarged by some boy's busy penknife. One day, with Watson's help, he manoeuvred his calipered leg on to the desk. The leg being without muscular stiffening, the manoeuvre caused him neither pain nor inconvenience. Then, through his pebble spectacles, he began peering down at the hole.

'Please, sir,' said Watson, with an uncharacteristic show of solicitude, 'I'm afraid there's something far wrong with McArthur!'

The master came bustling and chewing from his desk. 'What do you mean, something far wrong?' Then he saw the complicated position into which his star pupil had got himself. 'Good heavens, boy, get that leg down!'

McArthur gave no sign that he had heard. Watson said: 'He's stuck like that, sir. I think he's in a trance.'

By this time the whole class was moving and murmuring with excitement. That our parents were paying large sums in rates and taxes in order to provide us with a sound education – and that the time we spent in the Latin class was a complete waste of their money – did not occur to us. We were having a ball, free of care. A chorus swelled: 'Ah-h-h, bully! The poor maimed boy, don't touch him!'

It was what Mr Banks, the English master, would have called an impasse.

The Latin master chewed and muttered: 'MacVicar, you are his friend. Can you communicate with him?'

I could. I did, trying hard to simulate my father's sick-bed manner. 'Tell me what's the matter, David.'

He made guttural sounds.

'Please, sir,' I said, 'he's scared.'

'Scared? Of what?'

'He's got a phobia.' (This was another word we'd learnt from Mr Banks.)

'Oh, dear!'

'He's scared he's going to fall through that knot-hole. Putting his leg on the desk is a kind of defensive mechanism.'

Noises came from the class. They were compounded of stifled giggles from the girls and groans of satisfaction from the boys. Sweat began to gather on the master's forehead.

'It's incredible,' he said. 'Is there no way – '

'Let me deal with him, sir,' I said and went on: 'Tell me, David, what do you see down the hole?'

McArthur stirred. His voice came clear and powerful: 'I see the dark depths of Hades. I see great fires. I see people dancing round the fires. I'm scared! I'm scared!'

'Good gracious!' exclaimed the master. He may have suspected he was being codded; but in that age of amateur psychiatry, after Wold War I, he couldn't be sure. His body was tense, shaking.

'Don't be scared, David.' I spoke with emotion, because this was the part of the script that everybody was going to enjoy. 'You are safe in the Latin class. Your good and kind master is by your side.'

'Master, master!' breathed McArthur.

'I'm here.' The master caught the pupil's groping hand.

'Ah! The fires are dying. The people are no longer there. It's getting darker.'

'He's coming round,' I said.

We meant the coming round bit to be as protracted and enjoyable as that which had gone before. Unfortunately, at that moment, the bell rang for the end of the period.

'He's okay now,' I said, quickly, while Big Allan and Davie Watson, assisted by McArthur himself, got the leg down from the desk.

McArthur smiled up at the master and disengaged his hand. 'Thank you, sir,' he said.

'If you agree, sir,' I suggested, 'we'll bring something from the woodwork class and plug up that hole. We'll do it tomorrow in the Latin period.'

Tomorrow was another sunshine day.

The Latin classroom was next to that occupied by the English master, the redoubtable Alexander Banks, known otherwise (to us) as Kubla. ('In Xanadu did Kubla Khan a stately pleasure-dome decree...') The partition between them was of flimsy wood and glass, and at one stage a regular ploy of ours, when we became bored in the Latin class, was to strike our elbows against this partition, causing minor thunder-rolls. Big Allan, at one end of the row of desks running close to and parallel with the partition, would begin the operation. As the master leapt towards him, wielding the strap, the next boy would repeat the performance. And so it went, along the line, until the master pounced, breathing fast but still flailing, on Davie Watson at the other end.

This caper continued for several weeks until one day, during a particularly happy session of partition-bashing, a knock fell upon the door of the room. We stopped bashing. The master stopped flailing. He went slowly to the door, opened it and revealed Kubla standing there in awesome majesty.

'What is going on?' he inquired, making the sibilant lip sounds which always betrayed a high charge in his temper.

'Nothing, Mr Banks.' The Latin master was sycophantic. 'The desks are so close to the partition. Bound to be accidents...'

'May I come in?'

'Of course, of course!'

Kubla came in, adjusting his pince-nez. His glance travelled across the back row of desks. 'MacDougall, MacVicar, Watson,' he murmured. 'I might have known.'

A chill entered our bones. In the Latin class we were heroes. In the face of real authority we were cringing cowards.

Kubla said nothing more. He left the room with a curt nod for the Latin master. We became suddenly, painfully aware that we were due to spend the next period in the English classroom.

Immediately upon entering Kubla's domain, Big Allan, Davie Watson and I were told to stand by his desk.

He took out his strap – a beautifully clean-cut model,

seldom used. When everybody was seated, he said: 'I am going to punish you three boys as an example to the others. Your conduct in the Latin classroom is a scandal. It has now begun to spread, via the partition, to the English classroom. That I cannot – and will not – allow. Roll up your sleeves.'

With cold and clinical skill, and without the slightest evidence of passion, he gave us six belts each. As honour dictated, we did not flinch as the strap came down. We shut our eyes and endured. Afterwards, when red weals appeared on our wrists, we made sure they remained hidden. We were aware that our punishment was deserved, that there was no point in trying to behave like martyrs. Had other masters – or our parents – discovered the truth about the Latin classroom there was no saying what further disciplinary action might have overtaken us.

Having completed the execution, Kubla said: 'You will remain behind after school. I will see you here, in the English classroom.'

The day dragged by: a day sad, stale and unprofitable. At ten minutes past four in the afternoon we stood before Mr Banks, who addressed us. 'I am greatly disappointed in you – three boys from good homes, three healthy boys of intelligence and resource. Yet you act like louts, like hooligans from a mediaeval slum! You pander to your own pleasure, completely ignoring the rights – and even the very existence – of other human beings. Your understanding of a fellow mortal in distress is nil. Your compassion is nil. Your social conscience simply does not exist. Let me warn you that if this state of affairs continues you will find that when you leave school and have to face the hard realities of an unprotected life your chances of survival, in both a physical and a moral sense, will be poor indeed. Others will treat you as you treat them – and in this direction lie anarchy, destruction and the death of the soul.'

Kubla was not religious. His approach to the ethical problems of life was different from my father's, but it seemed to me then – as it seems to me now – that his basic philosophy was the same. And his words that day made us feel colder and more desolate than any fire and brimstone sermon had ever done.

For days afterwards the Latin class was fairly quiet, and I think we intended to show some compassion for the master. But before our goodwill could flourish he was removed from the school. This happened only a few weeks before we were due to sit our Highers. We passed English and Maths – 'nae bother', as we told one another – but as far as I can remember, only three out of a class of about twenty passed their Latin exam. One of them was McArthur.

In years to come the happenings in the Latin class made us all feel ashamed. Our behaviour was thoughtless, inhuman, on a par with that of the morons – amongst both players and spectators – who have devalued the good name of football around the world. We played a game which gave us selfish pleasure. That other people might be hurt and humiliated did not worry us – that is, until Kubla delivered his homily.

I have not mentioned the Latin master's name. He may still be alive, and to identify him would be cruel. But though McArthur is now dead, Big Allan in Campbeltown and Davie Watson in Perth will vouch for the truth – the conservative truth – of my stories about him.

They are proof, if proof is needed, that without discipline even 'respectable' children can menace society. Children are natural sadists. It is only by example – and, perhaps, under a threat of retribution – that they learn to become sympathetic human beings, with a reverence for the divinity in all other human beings, no matter how much that divinity may be camouflaged.

From our parents – and Maimie – Rona, my brothers and I learnt that love for our neighbours and respect for their dignity help to support a caring society and make us feel good within ourselves. From Kubla we learnt that punishment of one sort or another is inevitable if cruelty, hate and arrogance are allowed to take over.

From Kubla I learnt something else: that good writing requires not only integrity but also a great deal of disciplined work. Most week-ends he gave us an essay to write. At first I regarded this as an enjoyable chore. Ideas, and words with which to clothe them, came easily as far as I was concerned. (On many a Friday night I wrote two essays, my own and one for Watson, while he in turn did homework in maths for me.) But Kubla was not impressed by my facile imaginings, as a rule awarding me fewer marks than those he gave to other pupils whose writing I classed privately as stodgy.

I was annoyed with him. My scribblings became more and more florid in style and content. I searched *Chambers's Twentieth Century Dictionary* for bigger and, as I thought, better words. Fanciful theories were deployed at the expense of sober reason.

One day he returned my essay. It was marked 5 out of 10. On the margin, in his scrawling handwriting, he gave a verdict: 'The idea is good, but the writing is WOOLLY. The words, instead of being simple and straightforward, are too big for their boots. The composition is careless, the product of a mind too idle to think things through. You have potential as a writer. Why waste it in a cloud of vanity?'

To begin with, I was angry. Then I was depressed. Then I remembered the sentence: 'You have potential as a writer.' It was a flickering light on a winter sea.

Fortunately I understood what Kubla meant, though it was hard to admit the propriety of his judgement against my own. (Even yet, in mature age, I find that an honest valuation of adverse criticism is a difficult, even painful exercise.) The next week-end I laboured long and hard by the light of a paraffin lamp on the Manse kitchen table, choosing simple words for my essay and a simple argument which I did my best to bring to a conclusion. As he handed this one back Kubla gave me a fleeting smile and said: 'Better.'

Praise from Kubla, however curt and ambiguous, was praise indeed. I glowed. I wrote voluntary essays. I tried my hand at short stories, most of which I burned, because as yet I hadn't the nerve to offer them to the magazines and newspapers whose siren calls beckoned me from beyond a far horizon.

Eventually Kubla was marking my essays at 8. And then,

on one glad day, he gave me 9.

He said: 'I will read this essay to the class. Listen carefully and tell me, at the end, why it doesn't quite get full marks.'

My pleasure was drowned in a flood of embarrassment. It was gratifying that my work should have Kubla's approval. That my essay should be read out as an example to my mates was a disaster. Big Allan and Watson and Tom Wylie would make my life a misery. I should be called 'Kubla's pet'. I should be accused of 'sooking up' to a teacher, the most unpardonable of schoolboy sins. The girls might decide I was a cissy – or even worse, a 'swot' – and the glowing halo of heroism which their eyes accorded me in the Latin class might suddenly dim.

I sat and blushed and sweated, while Watson, beside me, dug an elbow into my ribs and Big Allan and Tom Wylie, seated at the desk behind, bent forward and surreptitiously tried to pluck hairs from the back of my knees. (In those days, more than fifty years ago, boys at school wore short trousers until they were seventeen.)

My essay was about a ploughing match: about the heaving, brightly harnessed Clydesdale horses and the glint of the brown earth as they pulled the sharp plough through and turned it over; about a grey January sky tinged with sunset pink and the horses and the ploughmen silhouetted against it; about the wisdom and the drams exchanged by ancient, retired ploughmen under rattling hawthorn hedges.

I heard only snatches as Kubla read it, being too busy fending off – and camouflaging – the painful attacks on my hairy legs.

Finally the ordeal ended. 'Well,' said Kubla, 'why did I deduct one mark?'

'Because it's a load of rubbish!' giggled Big Allan behind me, for my ears alone.

Renée Smith, who was kind and friendly, put up a hand. 'I think it's a great essay. But maybe there are too many adjectives.'

'You have a point there,' said Kubla. 'But you should have read some of MacVicar's previous essays. Every second word was an adjective!'

The class laughed. This was better. I was being brought back to a mundane average, where I wanted to be. The physical attacks ceased.

'In fact,' Kubla continued, 'this time he has his adjectives fairly well under control, a sign of some newly acquired discipline. No, I took the mark off for a sin of omission rather than of commission. Can nobody spot it?'

As a farmer's son Watson had attended the ploughing match in question. He ventured a cynical suggestion. 'He doesn't say anything about the dirt at the heid-rigs. I got my boots covered in glaur that day.'

'Good, Watson, good!' said Kubla, much to Watson's surprise. 'You're getting warm. There is certainly a touch of romanticism about MacVicar's work, though I don't necessarily condemn him for that. Realism can often be overdone. But in good descriptive writing there are, in my opinion, three main elements – sight, sound and smell. MacVicar deals with sights and sounds particularly well – the silhouettes against the coloured sky, the rattling of the hawthorn hedges in the wind. But he has omitted to mention the smells of the ploughing match: the smell of the damp earth – of the 'glaur' which you mention, Watson – the smell of the sweating horses and of their dung, the smell of the whisky in the cold air. That's why I deducted a mark from what was otherwise an extremely good essay.'

I soon forgot my embarrassment – and the prickling pains at the backs of my knees – but I never forgot Kubla's lesson. (Fifteen years later, when I had been taken under the wing of a literary agent, Patience Ross of A. M. Heath & Co., Ltd., she gave me advice on similar lines. As an example of how evidence of the three senses could be woven into prose she recommended me to read the *Natural History of Selbourne* by the Rev. Gilbert White. I discovered for myself that Lewis Grassic Gibbon was good at such weaving, too.)

And Kubla had done something else. He had confirmed my own suspicion that there was ink in my veins. I was still interested in athletics, football and cricket. I could still enjoy adventure in the Latin class. My ethical standards may have been improving, but, to borrow a word from Kubla, they still remained 'woolly'. Now, however, my main (if secret) ambition was to write something that would appear in print.

3. The Extra Dimension

I suppose the desire to write burgeoned inside me in parallel with the desire to make love to girls and to worship a caring God.

Psychologists have devoted libraries of books to analyses of the creative instincts, but I don't think there is anything complicated about them. They are born in every human being, implanted by a mysterious power as yet undefined in material terms. The sexual instinct – the instinct to create and nourish sons and daughters – and the religious instinct – the instinct to show gratitude to whoever or whatever has donated such gifts as we have – are common to everybody in greater or lesser degree. But alongside them each individual has other creative instincts.

The character of a person and a person's role in society depend a great deal on whether he or she is allowed to develop the more dominant of such instincts. Some are workaday, unspectacular. Others are of incalculable value to the human race. A few are dangerous. Knitting a jumper is creative. So is cooking a tasty meal. So is building a house, a motor-car or Rapides and Concordes. So is farming and gardening, painting pictures, composing music, writing books. So is the raising of business empires. But so, it must be admitted, is the construction of an A-bomb.

Those who find their freedom to develop dominant instincts – apart from sex and religion – are the lucky ones. They are the happy people, the fulfilled and, therefore, the contented people. The sad and frustrated are those who because of accident or inhibiting circumstances are unable to nurture their inborn gift and are condemned to labour at tasks which by no stretch of the imagination can be described as creative.

The Padre was lucky. His dominant instinct was to preach, and he became a minister of religion. My mother was lucky. Her instinct was to create a home and family, and she did just that.

Their family was lucky. Archie wanted to teach. He became an English master at Dunoon Grammar School. Willie wanted to be a sailor. He retired recently after many years as senior skipper with the Anchor Line. Rona not only wanted to teach, she also had an urge to sing. She taught in Campbeltown Grammar School, and in 1948, at the Mod in Glasgow, won the gold medal for Gaelic singing. Kenneth, like his father, had the instinct to preach. He became minister of Kenmore in 1950 and is still there, nicknamed the 'Bishop of Tayside'. John's instinct was to study medicine. He is now Professor of Midwifery at Leicester University. I wanted to become a writer, freelance and independent, and by guess and by God I did it.

The Padre and 'Granny' are gone, after long lives of willing service to their family and to the community of Southend. Archie was killed by a German mortar-bomb. Rona died of cancer soon after her happy triumph at the Mod. But Willie and Kenneth and John and I are still around. We can all testify that to be allowed to follow our natural bent is one of the most valuable gifts that parents can bestow.

The Padre and my mother wanted me to become a minister. For many years there existed an unspoken agreement that one day I should enter the Church. The impression was supported by my parents when, in my hearing, they spoke about me to friends and neighbours: 'I think he has a notion for the Kirk.'

As for my own feelings, I did have an instinct to preach as well as an instinct to write (if the two can be separated), an interest in the *Church of Scotland Year Book*, which listed in my books. Therefore I did not argue with my parents or rebel against their wishes and, indeed, at one stage took an interest in the *Church of Scotland Year Book* which listed Presbyteries and parishes and the stipends on offer. (It still does, unchangingly.)

I have to confess it was the stipends which interested me

most – an early pointer, had I but known, to my unsuitability for a Christian calling. At that time, in the early 1920s, one of the best rewarded ministers in Scotland was the Rev. D. Gillies of Kenmore. I remember that his stipend of £600, double that of my father, made my eyes pop. This will be my parish, I thought: I will be rich and famous and, in time, Moderator of the General Assembly. In the quiet countryside of Perthshire, too, there would be plenty of time to write my books. The idea that I might prove an inefficient or unworthy pastor did not enter my head.

(By a coincidence, it was my brother Kenneth who, in the fullness of time, became minister of Kenmore. Nowadays, however, as a result of reorganization, he is by no means the best paid minister in the Kirk.)

Meanwhile, however, my parents – more especially, perhaps, my mother – were interested enough in my attempts at writing.

From Mr Banks, the English master, the Padre learned that I was winning good marks for essays. (I seldom discussed school matters at home. Had I boasted about my 9 marks out of 10 I should have had to keep a balance by admitting the six belts I had received from Kubla, and that was one disgrace on which I had clamped a personal D-notice.) The next thing I knew was that Alec MacLeod, owner and chief reporter of the *Campbeltown Courier*, had been informed of my so-called talent.

He was a stout, chunky, clean-shaven man with a drooping expression which sometimes, by sudden magic, became a wide, mischievous smile. His solid reporting of town council and Presbytery meetings fitted the drooping image. The leg-pulling laughter in the *Courier*'s most famous column, 'Sparks and Flashes', were in accord with his smile. To my father he suggested I should try reporting the Armistice service due to take place the following Sunday at the War Memorial in Campbeltown.

In the 1920s, with World War I memories still poignantly fresh, services at memorials all over the country attracted many people. Apathy had not yet begun to frost the warmth, nor had the denigrating propaganda of those who had dodged the column of active service begun to have an effect. Even in Southend (pop. 500) scores of people would gather at the cross-topped cairn at Keprigan and bow their heads in silent gratitude for sacrifice. Today, after another world war and with a second memorial tablet added to the first, services in Southend are attended by only about a dozen folk, most of whom are close relatives of the dead.

This is not to say that on Armistice Sundays the Southend Church is empty. It is generally full and poppies glow in numerous lapels. But an effort is required of old sweats like Hamish Taylor, Archie Cameron and myself to keep the memorial from becoming isolated and neglected. Younger folk, concerned about the price of milk and cattle and the EEC agricultural policy, about striking power-workers and recalcitrant miners' leaders, about the cost and complications of modern technology, find it difficult to concede the importance of bygone wars.

Men died. So what?

But I think if we forget the men who died to preserve our liberty we will also be inclined to forget Christ, who died not only for liberty but also for love. And if Christ's message is eroded by inaction then the whole structure of our civilization will tumble back and down into pagan chaos.

The Campbeltown Memorial is tall and impressive, a tower of rough-hewn stone, situated on the Esplanade which crooks long arms around the harbour and the loch. Like the great religious edifices of the past five thousand years – the Neolithic and the Bronze Age chambered cairns, the crosses and the cathedrals, the churches and the yards about them – it faces east towards the rising sun.

On the day I carried out my first assignment as a reporter, the Esplanade was filled with people: kilted Argylls flanked by pipers and buglers; Scouts and Sea Scouts; Boys' Brigade members and Girl Guides; bemedalled ex-servicemen; crowds of doucely clad citizens wearing poppies – men, women and children. A minister read from St John, Chapter 15, verses 1 to 13, his rich voice trembling to a conclusion: 'Greater love hath no man than this, that a man lay down his life for his friends.'

In the silence the gulls wheeled and cried above the harbour. The water of the loch hissed over the pebbles on Dalintober beach. Then the exploding maroon broke the silence and the buglers sounded the Last Post, cold and clear, with its final note of heart-rending uncertainty.

The bustle began. The pipes skirled. I found myself in a maze of emotion.

I was only sixteen. So far life had been for jokes and pleasure. In spite of the fact that my father had spent a year in Salonika as a chaplain with the Lovat Scouts – thereby gaining his nickname, the Padre – the war had not interfered with my selfish interests in any serious way. Perhaps for the first time I realized that until now my research into living had barely disturbed the surface. Around me that day I felt an upsurge of love and pride and a determination to match sacrifice with sacrifice: love for the soldiers who had fought and won and for those whose names were black on the memorial; pride in Scotland for nurturing such soldiers, with their kilts and sardonic humour and 'gallus' bagpipes; determination to work and make patriotic sacrifices as some small recompense for what the dead had done for the living.

For myself, I understood at last how lucky we MacVicars were as a family to have the Padre back, safe and unscathed. Tears stung my eyes. To my neighbours in the gathering I could say nothing: my throat was dry. But words to describe it all tumbled in my head. I could see it – column after column in the *Courier*, by the up-and-coming literary star, Angus MacVicar. It spread out in my being like a tide, a masterpiece of reporting. The conception was wonderful. It shook me and left me spent as in the aftermath of an orgasm.

That evening I sat down to write. But now, with the paper before me white and blank and my new Waterman fountain pen poised above its surface, I found that only a trickle of words would come. I struggled to express the emotion I had felt during and after the service. The result was drab, inept, a pitiful garment for the original soaring idea.

I wanted to be regarded as a writer; but the conviction grew that the report on which I was working would do me no good at all in that respect. I became tense with frustration. Had I not been sixteen years old and, in my opinion, a man, I might have wept.

I worked on. My mother came into the kitchen at midnight. The paraffin in the cut-glass bowl of the table lamp was running low. She advised me to go to bed, because in the morning I had to cycle ten miles to school in Campbeltown and reveille, therefore, would be at half-past six. But I said I still hadn't finished my report and wanted to hand it in to the *Courier* office, complete, the next day.

'Poor Angus,' she said. 'Why do you get so worked up? You have plenty of time to learn to be a writer.'

The Padre came through, slippers slopping on the cement floor, on his way to his usual pre-bedtime consumption of health salts in the scullery. He gulped noisily, flung the spoon into the empty tumbler and came back to the kitchen. 'Go to bed,' he said. 'Put out the lamp before you go. Alec MacLeod doesn't want a masterpiece. Just a plain report.'

Maybe Alec MacLeod didn't want a masterpiece. But I did, though I stopped short of telling this to my father.

As the flame on the lamp-wick began to die I wrote my last sentence. I put the manuscript in an envelope and climbed the wooden stairs to the 'boys' room' above the kitchen. Archie and Willie were snoring peacefully, but I couldn't sleep. I had written about a thousand words, most of them desperate attempts to recapture the spirit of the service and in my heart I knew that where fires should have been leaping there was only smoking dross.

How badly I had failed was revealed on the following Thursday, when the *Courier* was published. My 'masterpiece' had been cut to pieces. Only about two hundred words remained out of my thousand, and these were concerned for the most part with names and organizations. And Alec MacLeod had given me no 'by-line'.

It was an ego-tearing experience – the first of many, I may say, throughout the next half-century – but then, as now, I followed an instinct to pick myself up, brush myself down and try again.

In her book about George Gissing, *The Born Exile*, Gillian Tindall describes the extra dimension given to a writer, a dimension which 'makes them what they are, subtly altering and colouring all their reactions and endowing them with a peculiar double vision. Gissing suffered as a writer, because writing is tiring, sometimes difficult, often lonely, but he would certainly have suffered many times more had he not had this extra outlet, this characteristic which all the time made him something more than just another highly strung, well meaning personality lost in an uncaring world.'

Gissing himself wrote: 'In the midst of serious complications in life I suddenly find myself possessed of calm and able to regard everything as a picture. I watch and observe myself as much as others. I can pause and make a note for future use, and the afflictions are to me materials for observation.'

As a writer I don't class myself with George Gissing; but I have come to understand exactly what he meant.

Archie and Willie and I had a friend called Tom Williamson.

Tom wasn't a tinker but, in modern statistical terms, one of the 'travelling people'. When we knew him he was about sixty, and rumour had it that he was an old soldier down on his luck. His back was certainly barrack-square straight and the look in his bright blue eyes was frank and direct. He had no beard or moustache, though the plentiful grey stubble on his face was clipped rather than shaved. He wore old tweed trousers, gathered under the knees with string, and layers of jerseys and cardigans. Out of doors his scanty grey hair was generally covered by a lady's knitted bonnet.

As far as we could tell he never touched strong liquor, though the story was that on being discharged from the army he acquired for a time 'a drinking problem'. (Then, as now, alcohol was a convenient peg on which to hang all kinds of social aberrations. That society itself – and its frequent lack of loving care – might have been to blame was a proposition gladly, even eagerly, ignored.)

Tom travelled on circuit, like a High Court judge, his territory being the whole of Argyll. Every three months or so he would spend a fortnight in Southend, making his headquarters in some friendly barn. More often than not this barn was at Brunerican, where the young daughter of the house was Jean McKerral. (Even when she was fourteen, two years my junior, I had an eye on her.) Her mother had recently died, so each morning it was Jean who cooked Tom's breakfast, after which he would sally forth with his battered tin box with its two pull-out drawers inside, to hawk around the parish packets of pins and needles, wire-rimmed spectacles, reels of highly coloured thread and cheap but, according to the girls, highly desirable brooches.

More than fifty years ago, in the country places, the 'travelling people' – including, of course, the tinkers – were given none of the social security benefits which ensure their comfort today. They were almost entirely fed, clothed and housed by kindly folk on the farms and in the 'big hooses' which they visited on a carefully planned rota. The money they earned from the repair of pots and pans and from the sale of trinkets, spectacles, bootlaces, needles and thread – and, in one case I knew, of potted ferns – was spent upon tobacco, drink and, sometimes, peppermints.

It was taken for granted, therefore, that at whichever house Tom happened to be around mid-day he would get a free dinner. The same thing held good at tea-time. For supper he returned to base at Brunerican, where, with the farm workers, he shared a great bowl of porridge, followed by piles of homemade soda scones plastered with butter and bramble jelly. He preferred milk to tea, so he got milk.

Jean remembers that on saying goodbye at the end of a fortnight's stay he would sometimes present her with a brooch, valued at about a shilling, in payment for his keep. She has a small collection of Tom's brooches still, and I have an idea they may be worth much more now than they were then.

Tom's dinner hour often coincided with a visit to the Manse. He would eat his meal in the kitchen, carefully handling a knife and fork under Maimie's critical eye. Then he would move out to the barn, where he would sit among the logs which awaited the Padre's devastating hatchet, fill and light a short clay pipe and exchange relaxed conversation with my brothers and myself.

I was particularly interested in Tom, because local talk insisted that he was 'weel educated'. He spent much of his time reading and always carried about with him a canvas bag full of books and magazines. Many of those were given him by wealthier 'clients' such as the Campbeltown distillery owners whose mansions provided a rich icing around the stodgy cake of the town.

One day my brothers and I, prospecting for fish in the river below the glebe, found Tom sitting on the wooden bridge which served the 'shooters', the smart businessmen from the south who, each autumn, rented the shooting and fishing rights from the Duke of Argyll. He dangled his legs from the tarry planks, contemplating the clear brown water below him. As usual he was smoking a clay pipe, the stem of which had broken off less than two inches from the bowl.

We sat on the bridge beside him. There was quietness, except for the occasional swirl of water on a partly submerged boulder or the distant cackle of a grouse on the higher ground above Kilblaan. Around us was an autumn scent created by decaying leaves and fallen crab-apples on the river bank and by late-flowering whins and brambles, yellow and white, on the path down from the Manse. The air was mild, containing only a hint of late-year chill.

'Looking for fish, Tom?'

'No. Just thinking.' His voice was deep, with gravel in it, his mode of speech deliberate. In contrast with our Kintyre brogue, his accent was almost artificially 'correct'.

That he should be thinking about anything other than fish in his present situation sounded incredible to us. Already we could see a salmon lying beside a green-slimed rock, speckled and sleek and lazy, facing upstream. Legally, of course, it belonged to the 'shooters', but had Tom not been there Archie and Willie and I might have attempted a take-over bid.

'What are you thinking about, Tom?'

'Did you ever hear of a poet called Swinburne?'

I said yes, having listened to Kubla lecturing about him.

'He wrote well for an Englishman,' said Tom. 'There must have been a bit of the Celt in him.'

Then he recited the verse which has triggered off so many sermons, both Christian and agnostic, that it has become almost a cliché:

> From too much love of living,
>   From hope and fear set free,
> We thank with brief thanksgiving
>   Whatever gods may be
> That no man lives forever,
>   That dead men rise up never;
> That even the weariest river
>   Winds somewhere safe to sea.

Was Tom letting Swinburne speak his own thoughts? At the time my brothers and I missed the implication, because an old sad man's philosophy was beyond our comprehension. We were, all three of us, in love with life; we were buoyed up by hope though, admittedly, sometimes beset by small fears; we were in no hurry to reach the safety – and dark oblivion – of the sea. It was true that a happy life depended on looking forward: our parents had taught us that much. But for us it was more adventure, more excitement, more loving that we looked forward to, not a blank 'nothingness'.

Perhaps Tom, studying our faces, realized that we were on different wavelengths. He took the broken pipe from his mouth, spat into the river twenty feet below and smiled across at us.

'When you get old,' he said, 'you'll experience sadness, as Swinburne did. As I do, too. But you recover from it. I think life is enjoyable at times. Like now, with the weather mild and the smell of autumn in the air, and the peaceful river.'

He had a schoolmaster's grip on us. We murmured responses and let him speak.

'In the winter, when it's cold, I look forward to days like this. But that's not much to keep a man going, is it? If I had my life to live over again I would be a farmer or an inventor or maybe a writer. The farmer has to plan his crops years ahead, and so the future for him is always interesting. Same with the inventor. Will he be able to patent his invention and make a fortune? While a writer works on a book he can dream about it being published and having an influence on other people. A farmer, an inventor or a writer, if they fail at times they don't see it as the end of the road. They have the next crop, the next invention, the next book to look forward to.'

'For them no weary river?' I said, or youthful words to that effect.

'Well, let us say a river that is less weary.'

Archie said: 'The way you talk, Tom, you should have been a minister. Then you would have Heaven to look forward to.'

His wry smile vanished. He frowned. 'Aye, maybe,' he said.

He got up and hoisted the tin box to his shoulder, indicating that our audience was at an end. Something had upset him. What it was we couldn't understand.

Next time we met, however, he retained none of this mood. I gave him a *Hutchinson's Magazine* in exchange for a tattered copy of *The Strand*. I found there a Bulldog Drummond story and thought: little does H. C. MacNeile realize that hundreds of miles from London, down at the Mull of Kintyre, a young rival is flexing his muscles for a fight. Compared with that exciting idea Tom's psychological problems were, to me, of small importance.

One summer he failed to appear in Southend. We never saw him again. Nobody in the parish could tell what had happened to him. To this day, though I have made many inquiries, I still cannot tell.

I hope his journey had a happy ending, undisturbed by the callous ignorance of youth.

For a long time Tom's magazines remained piled under my bed in the 'boys' room'. My mother and Maimie would have thrown them out, for reasons of hygiene. But I explained that I wanted to re-read them as a guide to how saleable stories ought to be written. Faced by such a professional attitude, they allowed a stay of execution.

The Padre classed most of the magazines – with the excep-

tion of *The Strand, Blackwood's* and *Chambers's Journal* –
as rubbish and advised me to select my reading from the
more solid books in his library.

Fifty or sixty years ago, in Southend, books were hard to
come by. There was no lumbering pantechnicon packed by
the District Council with up-to-date literature and labelled
'Mobile Library'. Campbeltown had one or two small shops
which depended for their profits mainly upon newspapers,
stationery and cigarettes but which also sold books – that is,
if paperback 'love romances' and adventure stories featuring
Dixon Hawke and Sexton Blake could be described as such.
In the country, if anyone ever bought a book, it was usually
from a travelling salesman touting 'bargains' like *Chambers's
Encyclopaedia* and *The Illustrated History of the Great War*
in twelve volumes (two years to pay) or from a colporteur
(we pronounced it 'colprature'), whose stock consisted generally of religious tracts but who, if requested, would take
orders for secular books.

One of these colporteurs was called Ambrose. My
brothers and I were mildly curious as to whether this was his
Christian name or surname, but we never found out.

He would be about fifty, we imagined. Clad as a rule in a
threadbare, tightly buttoned brown suit, he was flabbily
built, with a broad, pale clean-shaven face. It appeared that
he suffered from asthma, and we felt sorry that in order to
earn a living he should have to pedal such a heavy bicycle –
and an even heavier caseful of books – all round weather-
beaten Argyll.

Ambrose's main port of call in Southend was the Manse,
which he often visited just about tea-time. Unlike the tinkers
and the peddlars who ate in the kitchen, he joined the family
at the tea-table and rewarded us with erudite conversation
regarding his trade.

(Another regular visitor accorded similar status was
Campbell, the piano tuner, a round, ruddy-faced bespectacled Pickwick of a man, who, on finishing his job, always
delighted my mother with a spirited recital of Highland airs,
for her a more than adequate recompense for his meal.)

After tea, Ambrose and my father would discuss books.

Archie and Willie, younger than I and less interested, would adjourn to ploys of their own in the 'boys' room' or in the barn; but I always sat in to listen as the two bibliophiles talked by the dining-room fire.

It seemed to me that their main enthusiasms were for Sir Walter Scott and Charles Dickens. Jane Austen, William Makepeace Thackeray and Thomas Hardy were also mentioned in reverent terms, as was George Eliot, who, they revealed to me, was actually a woman, a Mary Ann Evans who later became Mrs J. W. Cross.

As far as I remember, the only contemporary author who found some favour in their eyes was A. S. M. Hutchinson, whose novel, *If Winter Comes,* was among the first of the modern 'best-sellers'; Once I heard my mother say that she liked stories written by Berta Ruck, but they scoffed her into smiling silence.

The Padre's library contained well-bound copies of the works of Scott and Dickens, two separate gifts from the Dowager Duchess of Argyll, who happened to be a member of his congregation. It also included *The Pilgrim's Progress*, *Pride and Prejudice*, George Borrow's *Lavengro* and James Boswell's *Life* of Dr Samuel Johnson. I tried to read them all but could discover in myself no spark of the enthusiasm displayed by my father and Ambrose. With the exception of Scott's *Tales of a Grandfather*, which includes a stirring description of the fight between Clan Chattan and Clan Kay on the Inches of Perth (enough to satisfy any boy's natural lust for violence), and of Dickens's *Christmas Carol*, mercifully short, I found them difficult, to say the least.

I had – and still have – a lazy mind, and this may have caused in me a blindness for genius. But the long descriptive passages and involved philosophical arguments with which most of them are upholstered seemed to me superfluous, a handicap to the flow of action. If ever I write a novel, I thought – and even then I was certain that one day I should – it will contain no such padding. The characters and their actions will speak for themselves; the main consideration will be the narrative.

In a more modern age, films, radio and television have

demonstrated that behind all the verbiage Scott was a magnificent storyteller, with a deep insight into the Scottish character, though it may be argued that his portraits of English men and women are sometimes dim and cardboardy. They have also demonstrated that when stripped for continuous action Dickens's characters are the very stuff of drama and that he, too, was no slouch where plots are concerned. I only wish that the publishers of Scott and Dickens had stipulated in their contracts that each of their novels should consist of, say, 60 000 words instead of the hundreds of thousands which straggle endlessly across pages and cause most young people to stop reading before the narrative takes hold of them.

I feel warm sympathy for those writers who have adapted Scott and Dickens for the media. Their dedication and hard work – and their ability to remain clear-headed while plodding through wordy morasses – make me ashamed of my own inadequacy.

A recent number of the Winchester College magazine has confirmed a suspicion that my youthful allergy to certain 'classical' authors is by no means unique. It published a census of home reading by fifth-formers who not only named their unfavourite authors in order of precedence but also listed the most boring books imposed upon them by well-meaning masters.

Dickens topped the poll of unfavourite authors, followed by Jane Austen, George Eliot, John Bunyan, Thomas Hardy, Joseph Conrad, James Boswell and Tolkien. (In my youth Tolkien's fantasies hadn't emerged upon the literary scene like a religion; but, having read him in mature years, I must agree with the Wykehamists that he is worthy of his place.)

In that list there is only one author whose inclusion I would question, personally. He is Joseph Conrad. I reckon that any boy with a proper mixture of salt in his veins will find Conrad's *Typhoon* anything but boring. Girls may not be so enthusiastic, because of its strong masculine qualities; but they ought to discover merit in the characterization of the old Scots engineer, McWhirr.

The Wykehamist list of boring books runs from *Pride and Prejudice* through *Pilgrim's Progress* and *The Mill on the Floss* to *Great Expectations;* and again I have to admit that my prejudices are generally in tune. Indeed, while at school – and at Kubla's insistence – I started to read *The Mill on the Floss* on at least three occasions and got hopelessly bogged down each time. Twice since then, as a responsible adult, I have tried reading it again, only to find that after the first chapter other interests have invariably called me away – lively interests such as amateur drama or a game of golf.

I am surprised that the Winchester fifth-formers omit Scott from their lists. Perhaps they do not know about him, their education being somewhat thirled to the English ethos. In that case, they have been spared, unwittingly, more mental weariness – though to be fair, I did dredge up some boyish pleasure from *Guy Mannering*, a story about the Solway smugglers. And I repeat that *Tales of a Grandfather*, if persevered with, yields a satisfactory crop of mayhem.

'I doubt,' said Bruce, 'that I have slain the Red Comyn.'

'Do you leave such a matter in doubt?' said Kirkpatrick. 'I will mak siccar!'

In fact, though in the Waverley Novels Scott did write great hunks of boring prose – and which of us hasn't, in our time, pressed and depressed by looming overdrafts? – I still have a warm regard for him, both as a writer and a man. His poetry combines robust narrative with lyrical passages of haunting, delicate beauty, and there is nothing boring about the bustling rhythms of his writing in *The Lay of the Last Minstrel*, *Marmion* and *The Lady of the Lake*.

After Scott's death, Lord Cockburn, the great Scottish judge, wrote vividly and movingly of his personality: 'Dear Scott! . . . It is a pleasure, which the next generation may envy, that I can still hear his voice and see his form. I see him in the Court, and on the street, in company and by the Tweed. The plain dress, the guttural, blurred voice, the lame walk, the thoughtful heavy face, with its mantling smile, the honest, hearty manner, the joyous laugh, the sing-song feeling recitation, the graphic story – they are all before me a hundred times a day.'

Born in 1771, one of a family of nine (of whom only four survived infancy), Scott had poliomyelitis as a baby, which left him with a limp. But in spite of this handicap he loved the country and its athletic pleasures. At Abbotsford he 'could ride and walk longer distances than most of his friends'. He called himself a 'rattle-skulled half-lawyer, half-sportsman' and was at pains to acquire the image of a country laird rather than that of a professional writer. To this end he often toiled in his study from about five o'clock in the morning until after breakfast-time, after which he mingled with his guests in the role of a carefree aristocrat with no need to engage in vulgar work.

There was another unusual – and, to me, engagingly human – side to his nature.

He was a regular reviewer of books for *The Scots Magazine*, and it has been discovered that he himself was the anonymous critic of *Ivanhoe*, analysing, quoting and interpreting the novel in an article stretching, characteristically, to several thousand words. He had no inhibitions about describing the story as 'masterly' and the author as 'the enchanter who peoples every region of fiction with the delightful creations of his unwearied and exhaustless (*sic*) fancy'.

A year later he published *Kenilworth* and readers of *The Scots Magazine* were advised by the same anonymous critic to regard Scott as 'the greatest genius of the age . . .who has already paid to the full all the debt to his country which her most devoted children would require'.

I have a fellow-feeling with Scott. When my first book, *The Purple Rock*, was published by Stanley Paul in 1933 I was asked – as is usual in the trade – to supply a draft blurb for the jacket. Without hesitation I did so, in the following terms: 'For sheer excitement and dramatic tension there are chapters in this novel which have seldom been surpassed in modern fiction. *The Purple Rock*, however, is not a "thriller" of the conventional type. Shrewd yet kindly humour, the competent portrayal of a group of highly original characters, and descriptive passages having a real literary value help to make it one of the most readable and entertaining books ever written by a Scottish author . . . The plot is worked up to a tremendous climax.' Probably in a daze of astonishment, my publisher, Frank Cowling, decided to use my 'blurb' without the change of even a comma.

Reading it over today, forty-five years on, I shiver with embarrassment; and perhaps it was lucky for me that in 1933 there was no Trade Descriptions Act. But in a way I can excuse myself, as I can excuse Scott for similar behaviour. A writer needs encouragement. For the sake not only of his self-esteem but also of his self-image he requires regular recognition that he *is* a writer. If nobody else seems willing to offer such inspiration then he is impelled by his own burning ambition to do it for himself.

But such lightsome aspects of Scott's character were more than balanced by his capacity for hard work and by his strong sense of pride and responsibility. His poetry having brought him fame and a flirtation with wealth, he began to live in the lairdly style which he enjoyed. Then, without warning, disaster came. His partner and publisher went bankrupt, leaving Scott penniless and in debt. But he wasted no time in self-pity. Refusing to take refuge in a bankruptcy of his own, he settled down to work as he had never worked before; and during the next few years, while producing many of the Waverley Novels, he paid off all his debts and became solvent – and independent – once again.

Though from 1821 until his death in 1832 he held literary and social court at Abbotsford, his country house in Roxburghshire, he did not die a rich man. But I reckon that in the end he achieved his ambition, living the kind of life he wanted, in gracious surroundings, owing nobody.

I suspect it was this aspect of his character, even more than his writing, which appealed to my father and Ambrose. They were both men of independence, who, like the majority of Scots, considered independence a main ingredient in the good life. (Though he lived long enough to contemplate its benefits, the Padre was always suspicious about the Welfare State. 'Makes people stop trying,' he used to say.)

In spite of his enthusiasm for the so-called 'classics', however, Ambrose took my side when I suggested that a few modern books might enhance the value of the Manse library. To my delight the Padre, albeit somewhat reluctantly, agreed.

Between us, from a small, grimy catalogue which Ambrose produced from his case, we chose a list of about a dozen books, all well bound hardbacks at half a crown apiece. The total cost was approximately thirty shillings; and if that seems a tiny amount, it has to be remembered that in the 1920s my father's annual stipend was only £300, less than a twelfth of what the minister of Southend earned in 1979. For the same number of cheap books today the Padre's successor would be faced with a bill for £17, no small sacrifice for a man responsible for the care of a large family and an eleven-roomed Manse.

But as one whose birthplace was a smokey 'black house' in North Uist, where the only light in winter was a *cruiskean* (a small dish of oil with a wick in it) and where the only reading matter comprised the Holy Bible, the Shorter Catechism and an occasional Gaelic number of the Church of Scotland magazine, *Life and Work*, the Padre always possessed great love and respect for books and was determined that his children should benefit from a catholic choice of reading, something denied to himself when young. Just before he died in 1970, aged ninety-two, he presented each of his surviving sons with a copy of the Oxford *Dictionary of Quotations*. 'It contains the wisdom of the ages,' he told us. 'You'll all find it useful when I'm gone.' (Of course, he regarded himself as our oracle so long as he remained alive; and I think my brothers will agree with me that he had sound reasons for doing so.)

The authors whose works I chose from Ambrose's catalogue were, however, comparatively unknown to him. From my point of view this may have been fortunate. But when the books arrived about a fortnight after Ambrose's visit I was glad to notice that the Padre, though inclined to mutter 'More rubbish!' on opening each one, read them all as avidly as I did.

Topping the list was Rafael Sabatini's *Captain Blood*; and I can remember the thrill of satisfaction and admiration that ran through me as I read the passage in which Peter Blood delivers his Parthian shot to Judge George Jeffreys of Wem. There were books also by Stanley Weyman, S. Walkey and Talbot Mundy. Later, when *King of the Khyber Rifles* was made into a film, the Padre admitted to me that he had enjoyed this particular book most of all. *Bones of the River*, by Edgar Wallace, was another of my choices ultimately approved by him, though today it would almost certainly be proscribed by the Race Relations Board.

That Owen Wister's *The Virginian* should have been included in the list was, I suspect, the result of the Padre (and perhaps Ambrose, too) confusing it with Thackeray's *Virginians*. But there was no confusion about Jeffrey Farnol's *Black Bartlemey's Treasure*. When my father read it he summoned me to his study and lectured me on the danger of reading 'such romantic tosh'. But I revelled in Farnol's lusty 'love stuff'. It produced a thrilling response in my adolescent body and made me dream excitedly of what I might presently do to some nubile and willing girl. It was the nearest I got to pornography.

Not long after providing us with the sensational 'new books' Ambrose ceased to visit us. There had been talk of his retirement from the road and of a journey to visit a daughter in Fife.

I wish I had discovered more about him. He had been well schooled. He was of a gentle, studious disposition. He had a weak chest and was inclined to stoutness. In spite of all this, how did he become a colporteur, roughing it in all weathers on a ramshackle bicycle and living, to some extent, on the charity of his 'clients'? Was he, by any chance, a 'stickit minister', a man with a calling for the Church who yet had failed to pass the divinity examinations?

When in Southend he always used to visit the ruined thirteenth-century chapel in Keil graveyard. One day, curious as always, Archie and I followed him on our bicycles. From a vantage point on the hillside above the roofless building we watched him go inside. On one of the ancient, recumbent gravestones he spread his waterproof coat, knelt care-

fully and stiffly upon it, clasped his hands against his forehead and began muttering a prayer.

Why, as we scuttled away, did I feel so disturbed, so
guilty?

4. Student Irregular

Sport has always been important to the MacVicar clan.

The Padre was the first captain of Glasgow University Shinty Club when it was founded in 1901, and he once played for Scotland against an Irish team. His skill with the *caman* (shinty-stick) was transmitted to my sister Rona, who, just before World War II, played lacrosse at the level of a Scottish International trial. It has also reappeared in two of his granchildren – Willie's youngest daughter, Susan, and John's eldest daughter, Marsali. Susan is a regular member of the Scottish Women's hockey team, while Marsali, an under-23 internationalist, has recently joined Susan in the seniors.

As yet, the male members of the clan have never reached such dizzy heights of sporting accomplishment; but Archie, as well as being a good left-handed golfer, was a soccer blue at Glasgow University, and Willie, Kenneth, John and I are all happy and reasonably successful golfers. (Five years ago I had a handicap of 5. This year, to my chagrin, they have hoisted me to 12. But on my home course at Southend – the famous Links of Dunaverty – which has a standard scratch of 63, I have recently acquired a new ambition – to do a medal round equal to or less than my age. It can be done. I have done it more than once in a friendly game.)

In our day, my brothers and I were all keen athletes. Our interest in running and jumping and throwing weights was first kindled, I think, at the Southend Sports, which, when we were children, took place annually on New Year's Day.

The New Year holiday, a blessed relief from laborious work on the farms, was always celebrated in Southend with feasting, drinking and jousting. Back in the nineteenth cen-

tury the jousting took the form of a shinty match between
teams of about twenty or thirty men from two rival areas in
the parish – Machrimore and Glenbreckrie. In the end, however, this degenerated into violence and fighting, until on
one sad day a young man died on the shinty field, head
broken by a blow from a homemade *caman*. After that the
shinty was no longer played; and many years later, in its
place, the New Year Sports were begun.

To us, as children, they afforded great excitement and
amusement; and, as I think back, it seems to me that the
weather was always sunny and dry, with perhaps a small hint
of frost.

No singlets, pants or spikes in those carefree days. For the
crack performers in the long-distance races the fashionable
outfit comprised a newly laundered woollen vest and long
drawers, vulnerable points secured with safety pins. The feet
were left bare and usually suffered no damage on the crisp
turf of the 18th fairway on the golf course, where the furlong
track was delineated by a circle of snare-pegs. Some of the
jumpers – and all the stone putters and hammer throwers –
wore tackety boots, in order to ensure a firm footing, and, as
a rule, they performed in shirt sleeves and 'gallowses'
(braces).

The great sprinters and jumpers were Willie McKerral,
Jean's second eldest brother, and Johnny Hunter. Stars in
the mile were Willie Balloch and Jim Russell, superb figures
in their off-white vests and long johns. The 'heavyweights'
included the Cameron brothers, John and Archie, men of
gigantic proportions to our youthful eyes and accoutred
strangely not only with fancy 'gallowses' but also with wide,
silvery buckled belts.

Shouts of appreciative laughter always greeted the
maverick competitors. Those were usually former athletes,
now in their middle years, who had started to toast the New
Year early in the day and were now stricken by genial and
adventurous drunkenness. When the Mile Race began they
would gallop ahead of the rest, shouting and waving to the
spectators, heavy boots thundering, only to collapse in heaps
before the end of the first lap. Nimbly Willie Balloch and Jim

Russell would leap over them, causing fresh outbursts of applause. The mavericks would then be hauled to safety by their friends and comforted by deep draughts from flasks or half bottles of whisky.

The Padre pretended not to notice. He was no spoil-sport on a holiday.

For us youngsters there was a sack race, for which each competitor had to provide his or her own sack. The great champion in this event was Davie McKerral, Jean's youngest brother, who sometimes arranged that small tears should occur in the bottom corners of his sack, so that his feet could move more freely. None of the rest of us had the brains even to consider such an idea.

By the time my brothers and I had reached the stage of becoming senior competitors, the New Year's Day Sports had been transferred to the summer. They are now called the Southend Highland Games.

The harvest of 1926 was late, delayed by rain and stook-tumbling equinoctial gales.

Having left school in June, I had spent the summer competing at all the local Highland Games – which included those at Southend, Tayinloan, Lochgilphead, Inveraray and Oban – along with my brother Archie, Hamish Taylor ('Boskers'), Lachie Young and Neil John MacCallum, who was the second son of the local blacksmith.

In the dressing-tents, in an atmosphere of embrocation and strange oaths, we rubbed shoulders with such great men as R. Starkey, the brothers Anderson from Dundee and J. McGregor from Spean Bridge. The only real professional among us was Neil John, who eventually won the mile at Powderhall and made a fortune for a few wise backers in the know. Archie, Hamish, Lachie and I were like small birds cleaning up after the vultures. In spite of all this, however, I had been able to collect about £20 in prizes, which I proposed to use as pocket-money at the university.

The Padre had also been busy on my behalf, acquiring for me a county council bursary of £30 and a Dundonald bursary, for prospective divines, of £40. Both would run for three years and allow me to complete a degree in Arts, *provided I passed all the exams*.

But here was the rub. It was the beginning of the examination trauma which has caused me nightmares ever since – a dream set in the Bute Hall of Glasgow University where I suddenly discover that the paper before me is covered with mathematical symbols, about which I know nothing, instead of the one in French which I have been expecting.

In addition to those bursaries I was also guaranteed, like every other student, an annual grant of £10 from the Carnegie Trust. I calculated, therefore, that my annual income for the next three years would be about £100 – that is, if I managed to win £20 each summer at the Highland Games. This seemed to me an excellent prospect; and indeed it was, being equivalent to something like £800 today. But, as will be shown, the whole financial edifice was as precariously balanced as that erected by any slick and daring City tycoon.

Euphoria, however, has always been a weakness of mine – though, paradoxically, in a writer it sometimes affords strength – and I faced the future with careless courage. And that autumn, as the harvest dragged on and the date in early October of my departure for the university made its relentless approach, I took another step which required even more brave optimism. I kissed Jean for the first time – on the dark side of a moonlit corn-stack at Brunerican.

I had been helping Jean's father and brothers with the harvest, not for money – at that time farmers had little to offer – but in order to be in Jean's company as much as possible. She was only sixteen, but her mother had died two years before and she was now mistress of the farm. I enjoyed coming in at night, after the day's work was done and the cart-horses had been 'lowsed', and sitting down to a meal of ham and eggs, followed by huge wedges of sponge-cake filled with whipped cream. The sponge-cake was – and is – Jean's speciality and my joy. I tried to imagine that occasionally she baked it especially for my benefit.

On the other hand, old Willie McKerral, Jean's father, and her brothers, James, Archie and Davie, seemed to consider my presence in the family circle as natural and unworthy of special note. Nor did they try to prevent me escorting Jean to certain dances and concerts in the Territorial Hall in the village.

I am afraid that as a dancing partner she found me as unsatisfactory as she had done six years before, when together we attended Mr McLeish's dancing class and the height of my achievement was to act as an immobile statue in the statue dance. I had many pangs of jealousy as she enjoyed military two-steps, Eva three-steps, hesitation and veleta waltzes, quadrilles and the lancers in the arms of more expert practitioners. But she was always willing to let me have the last waltz, a sign in rural circles that I had been chosen to 'see her home' afterwards and that eager rivals who might try to thwart me did so at their peril.

For helping Jean with the milking, morning and evening, old Barbara MacCallum was paid half a crown a week. She also had a cot-house free of rent and as much milk, butter and buttermilk as she needed for herself, her husband and a few adopted nieces and nephews. Barbara had a sharp eye. One night I waited for Jean at the top of the byre. Milk pail slopping, Barbara nudged me and whispered: 'She kens naethin' aboot it. But keep at it. She'll learn!' Her lewd expression made me feel embarrassed and even ashamed. I 'kent naethin' aboot it' either. All I knew was that I wanted to do more with Jean than just walk and talk and be kind. What that something was remained dark and nebulous.

The night before I was due to leave for the university there was no dance or concert, no obvious excuse to be with Jean. Then *she* had an idea.

A year before, Jean's brother John had married Cecilia, the youngest daughter of the Rev. George Walter Strang, minister of the Castlehill Church in Campbeltown. Together they had set up house at Dalbhraddan Farm, about a mile from the Manse. The marriage was full of singing and laughter. But then, at the beginning of summer, John's hand was caught in the gears of a turnip-slicer and he had died, within a week, of blood poisoning. Today, with the aid of penicillin and improved methods of medical care, such a tragedy would be unlikely to happen. But Cecilia had to face it, knowing that she was pregnant.

Young John McKerral was born in August. We didn't know that fifty years later he would be in charge of Modern Studies at Campbeltown Grammar School and a leading actor with the Dunaverty Players: all that occupied our thoughts at the time was that he and his mother should be given love and help by the family and the community at large.

That October night, therefore, Jean arranged to bring gifts of a chicken and some baby clothes to Dalbhraddan; and before any of her brothers could do so, I volunteered to carry her basket.

With a harvest moon shining down on us like a spotlight we trudged the three miles from Brunerican to Dalbhraddan. Jean went in, offered her gifts and saw the baby.

I waited for her at the bottom of the farm road. It was cold and clear. Silent, too, except for a tinkle of water in the roadside ditch and the occasional complaint of an owl in the fir 'plantin' ' half a mile away. Under the heedless stars, Southend lay rolling and dark against the moon sky. I was leaving it tomorrow, leaving Jean and my family and all the boys and girls who were my friends. Tomorrow night I should be among clustering buildings in Glasgow, for the first time alone against life. Why hadn't I been born a farmer's son, thirled to the earth of my native parish, able to earn a living in the kind community which was my birthright? Sadness flooded through me. A Hebridean sadness inherited from ancestors in North Uist who wept for lost homelands.

I fought against it, swallowing to ease the quiver in my throat. I would come back. I would write and make money to come back. There, in the whin-bush, the idea of becoming a minister was stripped of some glamour and impoverished.

An hour later Jean and I were trudging back to Brunerican, first along the main road and then by the side road which followed the burn. The cold sadness in the pit of my stomach had been replaced by another kind of primeval excitement.

'Trudging' is not, of course, the right word. I didn't even realize that I was walking. And though sometimes we staggered about on cart-tracks and loose rubble I kept my arm firmly about Jean's waist. She leant against me to keep her balance, and I acted the strong protector.

We scarcely talked at all, except about the baby.

'He's not very good looking,' Jean said.

'I don't suppose any of us was very good looking at two months.'

'I hope he doesn't grow up to be ugly.'

She need not have worried. As a juvenile lead in the Dunaverty Players, John became a notable heart-throb.

As we approached Brunerican I guided Jean away from the front door. She gave no sign of surprise. In the farmyard it was quiet, with the black moon shadows of the stacks like incongruities in a surrealist painting. In one of the shadows a pile of sheaves lay against the bottom of a stack. I put the basket away and put my arms about her.

She lay back among the straw and I kissed her. I must have made a poor job of it, because her response, from my point of view, was unsatisfactory. I felt her trembling, even crying a little.

'You're going away tomorrow.'

Characteristically, I refused to face reality and kissed her again.

Our trouble was the prickly corn-straws. Burns may have found no impediments 'amang the rigs o' barley', but I reckon that where non-poets are concerned passion is inhibited when sharp straws invade ears and eyes and noses.

But that night, without words, Jean and I knew that we wanted to be together for the rest of our lives. We promised to write to each other twice a week while I was away. And during the next four years we kept our promises.

As we parted she gave me a small silk handkerchief. Its colour, she told me, was heliotrope, and there was a touch of perfume on it. For the next ten years I kept that handkerchief in my pocket, below my own, and gave it back to her on the day we were married.

It was in a maze of half-understood love and home-sickness that I enrolled as a student at Glasgow University. An irregular student, as it happened.

In 1926 entrance to a Scottish University could be gained with three Highers and one Lower. Today candidates have to show a whole quiverful of A levels as well as numerous O levels; and even then, in order to 'mak' siccar', the pass 'bands' have to be well above fifty per cent. No wonder that in the past few years Glasgow University, for example, is facing a serious decline in its student population. The competence – even brilliance – of contemporary scholars fills me with admiration. Not long ago a young niece of mine who aimed not only to become a doctor but also to play hockey for Scotland carried off six A levels and three O levels, a feat far beyond my capacity.

All I was able to show after six years of happy education at Campbeltown Grammar School were two Highers, in English and maths, and two Lowers, in French and Latin. This was not enough for a regular enrolment at a university; but the director of studies at Glasgow was kind enough to suggest that I might enter as an irregular student for a year, taking degree classes in English and maths and studying French privately at the same time. If I passed the Prelims in French the following summer, along with the university exams in English and maths, then everything would be regularized and I could start my second year as a normal student.

I accepted his suggestion and spent the following winter and spring commuting between the University at Gilmorehill, Skerry's Commercial College in Bath Street and the University sports ground at Westerlands.

At Gilmorehill I sat under Professor McNeile Dixon in English and learned to appreciate a new world of literature and poetry, in which fiction writers – including Scott, Dickens and the inevitable George Eliot – were overshadowed by such as Beowolf, Henryson, Dunbar, Chaucer, Shakespeare, Milton, Burns and Keats. I felt the same thrill of excitement as had come to me while reading *The Rudiments of Criticism* and listening to the words of James MacTaggart.

All the time, however, another part of my brain kept insisting that a writer who wanted to make money – as I did – must not become too thirled to the higher flights of art. Only a genius, I argued, should indulge himself in such a way; and I was unsure as to the extent of my genius. I liked the world and its material comforts too much, along with the social and sporting side of life, to contemplate the ivory tower into which, it seemed to me, real genius must inevitably retire.

I considered the tall and lanky McNeile Dixon as a genius. Had I but known it, he was able to mix literature and the social and sporting life in an engagingly skilful manner. He was a golfer, who loved his weekly games at Glasgow Gailes and Killermont. The odd dram was another of his pleasures. But as he stood on his rostrum, lecturing to us on the subject of puritanism in literature, his sleepy eyes fixed on a point high above our heads, I had no suspicion that his own puritanism was liable, at times, to become diluted. To me, his utterances were god-like, and in my notebook I underlined with heavy pen-strokes his dictum that 'the touch of puritanism in the Scottish character is what has made Scotland a great nation, with a literature as strong and disciplined as any in the world'. At the back of my mind was the youthful hope that one day I might make a contribution to that literature.

McNeile Dixon's senior assistant was Dr Bickersteth, who specialized in Shakespeare. He was a small, round and untidy man, given to unexpected bursts of laughter. Male members of the class appreciated his bawdy jokes, which seemed to stem naturally from his absorption in the Elizabethan scene. But some of the girls declared themselves shocked by his 'coarse humour'.

One day three or four of them walked out in the middle of a lecture. As they hesitated at the door, his crumpled face, decorated with horn-rimmed spectacles, creased sideways into a smile. ' "Stand not upon the order of your going," ' he quoted at them, ' "but go at once." ' As they departed he turned to us with an impish look. Confidingly, and still lingering with *Macbeth*, he quoted again: ' "Away, and mock the time with fairest show: false face must hide what the false heart doth know." ' With deep laughter we young and sophisticated males registered immediate understanding of what the words implied; and our laughter swelled as he whispered to a few of us behind his hand: 'Let me offer a lesson of experience. The puritanical ones are always the best in bed!'

Dr Bickersteth's own private life was extremely orthodox, not to say puritanical, which could not quite be said about Professor McNeile Dixon's. It was odd, we thought, that the philosophies they preached should have been so contradictory.

I confess that as I look back over my own life I find in it echoes of McNeile Dixon's. I only wish I could have written a book like his principal work on literature, *The Human Situation*.

The English class was for me delightful. My essays, still written under the influence of Kubla Khan, nearly always got a beta plus. McNeile Dixon himself once gave me an alpha minus for a critical study of *Paradise Regained*, in which I disagreed with Milton's implication that God created Adam for God only and Eve for the lowlier function of serving God through him. This encouraged me to write an even more violent criticism of *The Pilgrim's Progress*. I described Bunyan's book as a crude fairy tale, unworthy of more than passing notice by powerful intellects. Did I convey the impression of some intellectual arrogance within myself? In any case, the essay earned me only a beta minus. Its marking taught me a lesson which emphasised not only the need for continual discipline but also the subtle dangers of swollen head. Sad to say, many editors and publishers can testify that I still have not fully learned it.

In general, however, there was no doubt in my mind that when the time came I could pass the degree exam in English. The class in mathematics was different.

At school, under the threat of George Hutcheon's baleful eye – and well-honed Lochgelly strap – I had worked hard and found the exams easy. Now, dependent on self-discipline, I became careless. The calculus was something that my woolly mind failed to grasp, and I had a feeling within myself that even though I did make a sacrificial effort and succeed in understanding it, the knowledge would be of no good to me as a writer.

It still hadn't dawned on me that a sound training in mathematics is of immense value to a writer – especially to a journalist. A mathematical theorem is set out on the lines of 'Given, To Prove, Proof, Conclusion'. What better structure for a story or newspaper article could possibly be devised?

I struggled with the calculus, but nearly always the struggle ended with my putting it aside and becoming happily absorbed in a book. One, for preference, by John Buchan, my new exemplar and hero. Towards the beginning of May 1927, it suddenly occurred to me that I faced disaster, because if I didn't pass in both English *and* maths, my university career would come to a summary end.

Meanwhile, in the afternoons, I attended the French class at Skerry's College.

Skerry's was a private institution, family owned. The place looked seedy, its dusty corridors covered with worn linoleum. Rickety wooden partitions, some with frosted windows set well above eye-level, created a maze of tiny classrooms. The atmosphere was drab, and it seemed to me that most of the teachers and students I met wore furtive expressions, as if all were intent upon covering up – and only possibly retrieving – past failures. Or was this idea merely a reflection of my own psychological condition?

And yet, in spite of appearances, Skerry's had a notable record of successful tuition. Budding secretaries and clerks and copy boys aiming for the higher flights of journalism were coached with great thoroughness in typing and shorthand. Young businessmen were groomed in the latest methods and procedures. And many, like myself, who had failed their Highers, were gently but firmly conducted towards 'Prelim' passes in several European languages. As the spring sunshine of 1927 percolated into the dull corridors I had begun to find a new interest in French, and *Pecheur d'Island* no longer proved a bore to translate.

At Skerry's I made no friends. People there were watch-watchers, counting the minutes as they hurried either to a job or from one. Time was precious to fugitives from failure. For myself, after the French class had 'skailed' I always rushed to board the blue tram-car for the Botanic Gardens. A penny-ha'penny ticket brought me into Great Western Road, across Kelvin Bridge and to the stop near Hubbard's, opposite Cooper's Clock. In the upstairs room at Hubbard's I would find my university cronies – Kenneth Tyson, James Davidson, Archie Robertson, Colin Mitchell – and there, as a reward for my labour at Skerry's, enjoy coffee and a chocolate biscuit (total cost, fourpence) and some happy argument untrammelled by time.

On winter and spring afternoons, when there was no French class, I often took a green tram to Westerlands, where Charlie Durning was in charge of training. Charlie wanted me to play rugby in the winter and start concentrating on athletics at the end of the season. 'You're big and strong and fast,' he told me. 'And a bit bull-headed. You'd make a grand three-quarter.' But I preferred soccer and spent my Saturdays playing for minor university elevens.

Donald McDiarmid, a farmer's son from Kintyre, was a senior law student at the time and also a leading figure in the soccer club. Even though my football skill was questionable, to say the least, he saw to it, being clannish, that I got plenty of games. He picked me once to play left back for the second eleven against a team from Aberdeen University. In the course of the game I scored against my own side, deflecting the ball away from the goalkeeper; I gave away a penalty by bringing down the opposing centre-forward with a scything kick and was eventually warned by the referee that if I used any more bad language I might be sent off. It was all disaster. I was immediately relegated to the fourth eleven, whose fixtures included games against precocious schoolboys and the inmates and staff of several lunatic asylums.

'I told you,' Charlie Durning said. 'You'd get on far better at rugby.'

But I never did like rugby. I dreamt Walter Mitty dreams of becoming a soccer star and being chosen for my country. The dream is still with me, and when Ally MacLeod's anti-heroes played in the World Cup I was with them on the fields of the Argentine, sweating and shouting and developing a stomach ulcer in front of the television set.

My ignominy as a footballer was thankfully forgotten when Archie, my brother, came to the university and retrieved the family honour by gaining a soccer blue. His 'blue' blazer now hangs in my wardrobe.

Donald McDiarmid played for the first university eleven, too, and won a Scottish Amateur Cup medal. Years later, when he became Sheriff Substitute in Argyll, he and I got together again, this time on the golf course. As a golfer I am less of a disappointment to him, except perhaps when, as sometimes happens, I beat him 'out in the country'.

It was as an athlete that I earned some approval from Charlie Durning. In my first year I ran in the two novice races at the university sports, coming in third in the 100 yards and second in the 600 yards. Charlie massaged my legs and in a haze of optimism and embrocation forecast that one day I should run in the 220 yards Scottish Championship.

This never happened, for a simple reason. Charlie and I suddenly realized that I was running at the university under false pretences. Because I had accepted money prizes at the Highland Games I was, in legal terms, a professional. If I wanted to run as an amateur at the university or at any other sports meeting arranged under the auspices of the Scottish Amateur Athletic Association I should have to apply for reinstatement. But I needed the money more than I needed medals. It was goodbye, therefore, to yet another dream.

I still have the medals I won for those two novice races at Westerlands, though I suppose that in strict legal terms I ought to have returned them. Should the SAAA or the university authorities now kick up a fuss I may surprise them by applying for reinstatement as an amateur even at this late date. And retrospectively at that.

I find that the word 'irregular' describes perfectly my first year at the university. And even after the summer exams it remained apposite.

I passed the degree exam in English and the 'Prelim' in

French. But in maths I failed, bemused by the calculus. It looked like checkmate.

At this juncture I remembered an article I had once read in an old *Strand Magazine*. It contained a story which the Padre often used as an 'illustration' in a sermon. The picture shows two men playing chess, one glum and despondent, the other moving his queen and triumphantly announcing 'Checkmate!' According to the writer of the article in the *Strand*, however, an expert study of the board reveals that the man who has apparently lost can still make a move and win.

Not for the first time nor for the last I found encouragement in this story. I went to see the director of studies, and sure enough, to my overwhelming relief, he indicated that a winning move on my part was still possible. I could re-sit the degree exam in maths in September. If I passed, then all would still be well.

That summer was a busy one.

The Padre growled and made frequent references to the fate of 'stickit ministers'. My mother kept telling him in Gaelic to 'let the boy alone'. Maimie, my brothers and Rona carefully avoided any mention of exams. Jean took the view that I must surely pass and was apparently unworried.

Peggy Taylor, 'Boskers' ' eldest sister, was a young maths teacher. During her summer holidays she gallantly volunteered to coach me in the calculus, and I worked hard to please her.

When I wasn't engaged in doing maths exercises for Peggy, or visiting Brunerican to see Jean, I trained regularly in the glebe (following a programme detailed in *Athletics*, the book written by Harold Abrahams after winning the Olympic 100 metres in 1924) and travelled with my mates to the usual round of Highland Games. All the time ideas for articles and short stories were turning and clicking in my head like computer wheels, but I tried to discipline myself not to think about them too much until I had 'regularized' my university year.

Thanks to Peggy, I am sure, the gamble paid off. I passed the September exam in maths, and a week before I was due to return to Glasgow I found myself at last a 'regular' student. It had been what John Buchan might have called 'a close-run thing'.

Entering my second year at the university I was in a happy mood. By a whisker I had avoided the full fury of the Padre's wrath. I had left maths behind me – for ever, I hoped. I had my bursaries and a sufficiency of money from the Highland Games. And in my pocket I had Jean's handkerchief.

This time I took classes in higher English, French and political economy. A cake-walk, I reckoned. And so it proved to be – at any rate in higher English and French. The Anglo-Saxon content of the higher English course caused me trouble; but Ritchie Girvan, who lectured in the subject, was a Campbeltown man, and this, for me, may have been fortunate. In the degree exam I translated *aetbrede* as 'wheaten loaf': it means 'nevertheless'. *Aetbrede*, I passed without further apparent difficulty. Inspired by Skerry's recent teaching, I made light of the French exam, too. But political economy was a fish of a different colour.

Anything to do with money and trade has always been beyond my comprehension. Sometimes I think it is beyond the comprehension of the so-called 'economic experts' as well.

Within recent years I have tried to follow their arguments in the public prints only to find that time and time again they contradict one another and, on occasions, even themselves. They prophesy a 'slump'. Out of the blue there comes an upsurge in trade, and from their published articles pessimism disappears like mist from a brae. They forecast great glory in oil. Then a 'slump' does come and they return to pessimism, reminding us with sadistic glee of their original prophecy. Oil, they inform us, has only about a decade to live. What happens then? Have they forgotten that in the 1960s they were saying exactly the same thing about coal? Now they tell us there is enough coal in our island to last for hundreds of years.

I voted for the Common Market, not for economic reasons but because I reckoned that any scheme designed to bring together people of different nationalities was a good thing. Some of the 'economic experts' who voted with me now bewail their 'mistake', because few advantages, money-wise, have occurred for Britain. In 1990 they may be singing yet another tune, though I am certain that money will still be their principal concern, not the moral well-being of ordinary folk.

I think it was the study of political economy at the university that made me sour and suspicious about economists. Laws such as those proposed by Malthus and Adam Smith appear to me still as depressing and unrealistic. Sounding infinitely wise in theory, in terms of human application they are as irrelevant as *The Naked Ape* to a young couple in love. I believe that any culture based on greed and a consequent manoeuvring for gain – as ours appears to be – contains a cancer which, in the end, will disfigure and destroy it.

Not surprisingly, I failed the degree exam in political economy. In September I failed the re-sit, too. The following year my subjects were moral philosophy and history. And political economy again.

Moral philosophy was a subject more to my taste. It seemed to me that it dealt with the problems of humanity as a whole rather than with the problems of a few wealthy people with money to manipulate. As an uncertain young man, uneasy and lacking in confidence, searching for solid belief, I found those parts of the course I could fully understand to be warm and comforting. I was fortunate in being able to sit under Professor A. A. Bowman, whose lectures, when read over and digested, tended to draw back dark curtains from my eyes.

I was lucky, too, in having a gentle, painstaking tutor in W. D. (Bill) Lamont. Only a few years older than I, Bill kept my spirits up with his impish humour and brought quick understanding of some – to me – obscure aspects of moral philosophy.

He and I had several common denominators. His father was a minister in Islay, mine a minister across the water in Kintyre. We would both rather talk and argue than concentrate upon making money. We both had a taste for canny Hebridean humour.

To illustrate a point I had missed in a moral philosophy essay, he told me the Gaelic legend of the Happy Man.

The King of Gaeldom, it seemed, was attacked by 'the black melancholy'. Court medicine men were baffled. None could effect or suggest a cure. In despair he consulted his chief druid, who, after a long and impressive silence, delivered an answer. 'Find a completely happy man, your majesty. Take the shirt from his back and wear it. Then you will find the melancholy lifting from your spirit like mist, and the blackness will become light.'

To every part of his kingdom the king sent messengers. Their orders were simple: 'Find a happy man and bring me his shirt.'

At first the messengers approached the wealthy people. But the wealthy people, though possessing many beautiful shirts, were all so worried in case they might lose their money, and so unhealthy in consequence of continually remaining indoors counting it, that none of them was happy.

Then they approached the wise and learned people, who also wore good quality shirts. But the wise and learned people were all so worried about their salaries and so frustrated by their failure to discover the ultimate secrets of life, that none of them was happy.

Then they approached the workmen and the labourers. But the workmen and the labourers, even though they all had shirts well designed to keep out the cold, were all so jealous of their wealthy employers and so upset because their dreams of living in a palace had failed to come true that none of them was happy.

Finally, however, a whisper was heard that in the farthest corner of the kingdom, on a little island off the beetling Mull, there lived a truly happy man. He greeted them with courtesy and pleasure, interrupting his fishing to invite them into his humble hut. (Today, after drawing his old-age pension, I reckon he might have been playing golf.)

'Are you a happy man?' they asked.

'I am, indeed. Completely happy. I live by hunting and

fishing. I am in debt to nobody, and nobody is in debt to me. I envy none. I love my fellow man and wish him well.'

The messengers were overjoyed. 'Then,' they said, 'in order to save the king from the black melancholy you will surely be willing to provide him with your shirt?'

The man wrinkled his sun-tanned forehead. 'I am sorry,' he said. 'You see me here naked as I was born. I am so poor in material things that I don't even have a shirt to put on my back!'

I enjoyed and admired Bill's story.

The following year, 1929, the new *Scottish Daily Express* erupted in Albion Street in Glasgow, in a dazzle of plate glass, cream-coloured cement and soaring sales. The editor was A. C. (Sandy) Trotter, then and for many years afterwards a good friend to young (and old) Scottish writers.

One of the first exciting features in the new paper was a short story competition, in response to which I composed a 'literary' version of *The Happy Man* and sent it in. To my joy it won first prize and was published in full. For many a night afterwards I took the paper to bed with me, to thrill at the sight of my name in prominent type, to re-read the story and, finally and happily, to say a prayer of thankfulness.

The prize was a beautiful grey and dark green rug decorated with the Celtic design of the endless snake. It had been woven in Lewis by unemployed fisher-girls, on whose behalf the *Scottish Daily Express* was running a campaign. I have it yet, the colours still bright under the tramp of countless feet in Achnamara's front hallway.

But the important thing was that Sandy Trotter had got to know about me. During the following ten years (happy, uninhibited years for non-staff journalists), which ended with World War II, I worked for him regularly as a freelance. He published my third novel, *The Screaming Gull*, as a serial and encouraged me to try short stories in addition to the usual bread-and-butter articles with titles like 'Has Highland Hospitality Grown Cold?', 'Stone Age Smokers' and 'Sour Milk for Sweet Old Age'. (This last one may have helped in a tiny way to make yoghurt popular.)

The *Express* Saturday supplement was my favourite hunting ground.

At eleven o'clock one Friday morning, not long after Jean and I got married in 1936, the phone rang in Achnamara. Sandy's voice came through. 'I want a twelve hundred word short story for tomorrow. Can you make it?'

'Sure,' I said, without hesitation, and put down the receiver.

Then I began to consider the snags. First, a new story had to be written, and I hadn't an idea in my head. Second, I had to get the typescript to Glasgow not later than 7 o'clock that same evening, and by road Glasgow is 140 miles from Southend. (At that time, for some reason, the phoning in of lengthy feature copy was discouraged. Nowadays I do it regularly, with a cheerful copy-taker egging me on.)

The answer to the second problem became clear at once. A morning and evening air service had recently started between Renfrew and Campbeltown, seven-seater de Haviland Rapides landing on and taking off from a field which bordered the road to Machrihanish. Sheep and cattle were herded away at the appropriate times, and passengers were weighed in at a little hut not much larger than a phone booth. On this particular day I remembered that the evening plane to Renfrew was due to take off at four o'clock in the afternoon. If I left Achnamara in my bull-nose Morris at half-past three I could reach the 'airfield' in time to hand my typescript to the pilot before he took off. He lived in Glasgow and would be able to deliver it at Albion Street before 7 o'clock.

The answer to my first problem depended upon another question. Could I conceive and write a 1200 word short story, correct it thoroughly and type out a 'fair copy' in the four and a half hours which remained before half-past three?

I told Jean about it. 'No lunch for me today,' I said. 'Just keep bringing me cups of tea. And let nobody near me. For the next four and a half hours you're the only one to know that I even exist.'

She sighed. She was finding it hard to sustain romance amid the realities of married life. I could see, however, that gradually she was coming to terms with the habits of a desperate writer. 'All right, dear,' she said and without further comment left me to my travail.

For the first half-hour I sat in an armchair by the fire, working out a plot. One came to me fairly quickly, because an urgent deadline is a stimulant even more powerful than whisky. (All my life I have favoured the idea that specific deadlines should be written into contracts, especially for books and radio and television work. Otherwise, as in my case, inherent laziness could take over and the project might never even get started.)

My plot concerned the adventure of a climber in Glen Croe, near Arrochar. He became lost in a blizzard but eventually, as darkness fell, found his way to a lonely cottage. Somebody – something – took him in. No lamp was lit; words spoken by the inhabitant of the cottage were slurred and indistinct, almost inhuman. Food and drink were given to the climber, but they did not comfort him. He shivered in the warmth of a peat fire, in the glow of which the other took care never to be seen.

I know. The plot is as old as the most ancient Highland *sennachie*. It resembles, too, as I later discovered, W. W. Jacob's story of 'The Monkey's Paw'. It revealed, finally, that the 'creature' in the cottage was a scientist recuperating after an accident in a chemical works. His face had been terribly scarred, so terribly that he could not bear to let anyone see it. And, of course, the climber turned out to be a plastic surgeon.

At the time I thought the whole idea inspired. In two hours I had written the story, in longhand in an exercise book. In another hour I had revised and corrected it. Half-an-hour's typing, followed by another half-hour's check on spelling and punctuation, and the job was done.

Jean came with me to the 'airfield' for the run, and thankfully the old Morris had no breakdowns on the way. I handed the typescript to an obliging pilot.

Next day, under generous headlines, the story appeared in the Saturday supplement. Sandy Trotter made no comment concerning it; but he sent me a cheque for £6 – in those days high payment for 1200 words – and that was comment enough for me.

I go into detail about all this because I believe it illustrates how much a writer's career depends on chance.

Had I not won their competition, the *Express* might never have heard of me and, in all probability, Sandy Trotter would not have helped to build my confidence and reputation by publishing so many of my articles, short stories and serials. And had I not heard the story of 'The Happy Man' from Bill Lamont in the moral philosophy class I would not have won the *Express* competition. A degree in maths enables me to add, *quod erat demonstrandum*.

Bill had an adventurous career. He left Glasgow to become professor of philosophy at the University of Cairo and for a time was principal of Makerere College in Uganda. But all the time the flame of his love for Scotland – and for Islay in particular – remained constant. Now, in his retirement, he lives in Glasgow, from where he and his wife Ann make regular forays into the West, pursuing their hobby of archaeology.

They often come to see us at Achnamara, to discuss the archaeological riches of Southend. I wonder if they know that my eagerness to help in their research is partly because of the debt I owe Bill for telling me about the Happy Man.

The story brought me material benefit. It brought me spiritual benefit, too. As did Professor Bowman's lectures, with their clear and unequivocal conclusion: 'There is a divinity within every man. Respect and reverence for this divinity is the foundation of civilized behaviour.'

When politicians denigrate one another, when demonstrators make violence, when the media resort to character assault – and even character assassination – in order to further the aims of the right or the left, I remember Professor Bowman's wise words and await, with some confidence, the ultimate triumph of the human spirit.

5. Divine Discontent

At the end of my third year at the university I passed in history and moral philosophy. With pale excitement I awaited the list of passes in political economy due to be published in the *Glasgow Herald*. If my name appeared I should have completed a degree as Master of Arts.

My name did not appear. For the third time I had failed in that dry, uninteresting, inhuman subject. My hopes of being capped at the graduation ceremony in June lay about me like melting splinters of ice.

That summer in the Manse was not happy. I felt that I had let everybody down: the family, Jean, the whole parish. The Padre seemed to agree with me. He had sympathy for failure when it stemmed from unlucky circumstances, but not for failure which he considered to be the result of idleness and a lack of application. My mother and Maimie were less critical, though the disappointment in my mother's big green eyes was a punishment even sorer than the Padre's frowns. My brothers and Rona avoided all mention of exams. So did Jean. But I heard whispers in the parish: 'If he canna pass his exams why does he no' go an' get a job in an office or something?'

An office?

Hopelessness gathered round me like a damp cloud. I wanted to write. I wanted to marry Jean and make a home for her in the country place and among the country people we both loved. But I had no money; I seemed to have very few brains, and the world gaped at me with neither encouragement nor compassion.

And I had developed acne. Shaving meant painful minutes each morning with a cut-throat razor – safety-razors were only coming into fashion at the time – while blood slid over my jaws and chin, staining the soap. This was followed by a squeezing out of pimply puss and an application of the zinc ointment recommended by my mother. I looked horrible, like a picture I had seen in a medical encyclopaedia of a youth recovering from smallpox.

I was afraid Jean might become disgusted with my appearance and begin to think about some of the clean-jawed young farmers who still, according to reports, crowded round her at the dances while I was away. I was depressed and only marginally comforted when my mother said: 'You'll grow out of it, Angus. And remember, if somebody loves you, the way you look makes no difference.'

One day, on the hillside behind the Manse, I lay alone in the summer sunshine, with the acrid, lusty scent of the whins around me, and watched a field-mouse emerge cannily from a tuft of grass. I contemplated my acne, my stammer and the turmoil of my academic career and knew how Burns had felt as he wrote the last verse of his famous poem:

> Still thou art blest, compared wi' me!
> The present only toucheth thee:
> But och! I backward cast my e'e
>   On prospects drear!
> An' forward, tho' I canna see,
>   I guess an' fear!

Apart from academic failure, I was now faced with the challenge of two new sprinting stars at the Highland Games. Their names were Duggie McEachran and 'Red' McGeachy. Sometimes I won – if I hadn't stayed out too late with Jean the night before. Sometimes both of them beat me; then, instead of a first prize of £1, I had to be content with a third of only five shillings. Archie and Lachie Young were beginning to beat me, too, at the high and long jumps. That summer the collection of £20 prize money was like a mirage retreating over the horizon.

'Red' McGeachy died some years ago; but Duggie McEachran still lives in Campbeltown, bright and breezy and quick. He and I like to foregather at a street corner to talk about our meetings during World War II in Palestine and Sicily, when he served with an Argyll 'beachbrick' and I with the Royal Scots Fusiliers. We also remember the old days at the Games. With ancient wisdom we discuss modern athletes and agree that they couldn't have lived with us. 'Result of the Welfare State,' opines Duggie. 'They're not hungry enough.'

But life went on. While studying spasmodically for yet another re-sit in political economy I also wrote articles and short stories. Most of them came back to me in the stamped addressed envelopes I was advised to provide. But some didn't, especially those I directed towards the St Vincent Street office of the old independent *Evening Citizen*, with its unusual pale green newsprint. I had discovered that the editor liked articles about the country, and I was only too willing to accommodate him. I sent him pieces of about 500 words dealing, for example, with the tinkers who helped with turnip-thinning, with the clipping and dipping of sheep on the upland farms, with the 'harvest home' and the custom of 'putting by' the last sheaf for the oldest mare's New Year's Day breakfast. He published most of them at half a guinea a time, which made up, to some extent, for prizes lost at the Highland Games.

Another of my markets was the *Scots Observer*, a weekly paper which had become popular under the editorship of the Rev. J. W. Stevenson, who later edited the Church of Scotland monthly magazine, *Life and Work*. Here again I had been introduced to an editor through the medium of a short story competition, in which my entry had been placed second to one by the distinguished writer D. K. Broster, author of *The Flight of the Heron*.

My story, 'The Keeper of Blaan', was the description of a poaching affair, inspired perhaps by Buchan's *John McNab*. It ran to 2500 words and was paid for at the rate of a guinea a thousand, the current rate for ordinary authors and journalists. Afterwards Jack Stevenson called on me frequently for more short stories and, eventually, for articles on current affairs in Scotland. One of those, concerning the tragic death of a Carradale man caused when a small fishing-boat was sunk by a basking shark, made a front page spread.

But then, in the early autumn of 1929, I struck what seemed to me like a 'gusher'. The editor of *Chambers's Journal* accepted a 2500 word short story which I had submitted in the normal way and offered me five guineas (i.e., two guineas a thousand) for it.

It was a 'humorous' story called *Vain Words*. The central character, the Rev. P. J. Macfarlane, an astute and rather cunning Church of Scotland clergyman, was modelled to a great extent on the Rev. D. J. Macdonald, the Pickwickian minister of Killean, a nearby parish in Kintyre. When hatching his nefarious plots, the Rev. P. J. always fingered the lobe of his left ear – a brilliant touch, I thought.

Some years previously, the Dowager Duchess of Argyll, our neighbour in Southend, had presented me with a book by Michael Joseph called *Short Story Writing for Profit*. It had become a kind of Bible for me, and had I studied my political economy text books with similar thoroughness I suspect I might have gained honours in the subject. Be that as it may, I had learnt from Michael Joseph that two guineas a thousand words was the average rate for 'professional' short story writers. The offer from *Chambers's Journal*, therefore, seemed to indicate that as a writer I might have 'arrived'.

Even in 1929 *Chambers's Journal* had an old-fashioned flavour. Compared with the bright, eye-catching covers of popular magazines like *Hutchinson's* or *Pearson's*, its printed, mustard-coloured exterior was drab. Like its contemporary, *Blackwood's Magazine*, it appeared to be aimed at oak-panelled clubs and twin-set country houses, though by the time my stories began to appear in it, I think the editor was trying to appeal to a wider, less conservative public.

Its production methods were also slow and stately, and I was disappointed when told that *Vain Words* would not be published for at least six months and that payment was due only after publication. However, all this was only a slight damper on pleasure. Six months would eventually pass. Then the story would appear and the money would come.

Something to look forward to. If I got the money now it would almost certainly be spent long before the six months had gone by.

It was my first formulation of a philosophy which I have been forced to adopt throughout my working life as a free-lance writer. Most publishers make up their accounts every six months and pay their authors the royalties on books sold during this period at the end of another three months. For example, if a copy of a book is sold at any time between July and December, the author does not receive the royalty on it until the following April.

Trade unionists with the benefit of a weekly pay-packet may look upon this state of affairs with horror. But let them hear this. One publisher for whom I have written children's books has a habit of keeping me waiting for eighteen months. When I expostulate – or when my agent expost-ulates for me – there is always a soft answer: accountants have been changed, computers have gone awry, some impor-tant person in the organization has been sick unto death. The unfortunate fact remains, from my point of view, that in this era of inflation money which comes in today is worth a lot less than it would have done eighteen months ago.

A freelance writer can never win a financial argument, simply because he has no powerful trade union to support him. He may be a member of the Society of Authors, but this ancient foundation, while its aims are honourable and it is helpful in the maintenance of high standards among profes-sional writers, carries no political punch. Since 1951 it has been trying to persuade the Government to pass a Public Lending Right Bill, by means of which authors whose books are lent out free by libraries may get some recompense. So far, in 1979, it has still not succeeded. I think the sooner it becomes a trade union the better, with leaders of the quality of Jack Jones or Joe Gormley who can make politicians sit up and take notice.

I often wonder what the Scargills and McGaheys of this world would say if their members were required to dig out lumps of coal for nothing so that the general public could borrow and burn them for free.

Of course, writers are on a bumpy pitch, as far as the use of industrial action is concerned.

One day, on the golf course, I was talking to a friend of mine, who is a printer. Slamming a rusty seven-iron into my bag after an indifferent shot, I said to him: 'Look at you with your £150 plus a week, paid on the nail. Look at me, with my £50 minus a week, paid sometimes eighteen months in arrears. And yet, what would you printers do if every writer in the country suddenly decided to go on strike?'

He laughed, selecting a gleaming pitching wedge from a brand-new bag. 'Don't worry, old boy. We'd still have plenty to do printing bingo tickets!'

Then he laid his approach dead and won the hole.

But in 1929, confronted with a bait of five guineas for my story, the implications for the future of payments both meagre and delayed caused me no anxiety. And presently more excitement occurred. One evening, returning to the Manse from a harvest day at Brunerican, I found that the post had delivered a bulky package from *Chambers's Journal*. The galley proofs of *Vain Words* had arrived for my urgent attention.

It was my first sight of galley proofs, but *The Writers' and Artists' Year Book* (and other published aids to journalism acquired with carefully hoarded pennies) had given me a fair idea of how to deal with them. Nowadays, beginning authors are even more fortunate. A table of symbols for authors' and printers' proof corrections, along with a guide to copy preparation, can be obtained on demand from the British Standards Institution (B.S. 1219: 1958 Recommendations).

As it happened, I found few errors or omissions in the proofs of the story. I showed the Padre my professional markings, and he seemed to be impressed. My mother made no effort to understand them. All she said was: 'I'm glad you're happy, Angus.' I returned the corrected proofs to *Chambers's* the very next day, dreaming a little of Abbotsford and a Rolls-Royce for Jean.

A few days later reality kicked me in the teeth again. Opening the *Glasgow Herald*, I found that my name still did not appear in the list of university passes in political economy.

And my acne flared up again.

The Padre made the decision.

It appeared that even without a degree I could enroll as a divinity student. While studying Hebrew, Greek and church history I could also attend – for the third time – the class in political economy. The Dundonald bursary, for budding divines, would remain with me, along with various others provided by the Church.

In my heart I was unwilling to become a minister. I felt unworthy to accept the challenge. I did want to communicate with my fellow beings, and to help them if I could, but from the pages of a book or newspaper rather than from a pulpit. If I did enter the ministry and take a stipend from the Church, the real reason would be that I wanted money to enable me to write: a mean trick for a shepherd to play upon an unsuspecting flock. But I lacked the courage to tell the Padre this. He had taken it for granted that I was eager to enter the ministry, and I baulked at the dangerous task of disillusioning him. And there was the sadness that would come to my mother if she discovered that her eldest son's principles were less holy and honourable than she had supposed. So, weakly, I let the situation drift. When the Padre laid out a scheme for a fourth university session I said I'd do my best to implement it.

That year, in the divinity hall, I rubbed shoulders with, amongst other brilliant men, Willie Barclay and Jimmy Dow, who, in the future, were both to become writers and broadcasters like myself. Even then I knew they were going places.

In later years, on a personal level, I lost touch with Willie Barclay, though, strangely enough, we both supported Motherwell Football Club. But I read all his books and listened to all his television broadcasts and, like a million others in Scotland, felt that as a result my Christian faith was strengthened. He possessed the secret of talking and writing with a simple clarity which left no doubt as to his meaning. His message was unambiguous not only to high-powered academics and practical scientists but also to cleaning ladies, farm labourers and youthful rebels. With his vast knowledge of Greek and Hebrew, he was able to give life to certain words and phrases in the Bible that had been muffed by the translators of the authorized version and by such means to bring vividly before us characters like, for example, St Paul: 'a wee man with a bad leg and a squint – and a chip on his shoulder'. No shining haloes or heroic holiness, just a 'wee man' with physical and moral weaknesses like the rest of us, who yet, in the end, gave up his life for his faith. When Willie Barclay died old Mrs Park in the village said to me: 'We'll no' get another like him.' She was right.

Jimmy Dow had the same gift of being able to communicate with people in both towers and tenements. He had a beautiful bass voice which he used to advantage in the pulpit and on TV – and also when he took the stage as an amateur actor with the Greenock Players. He translated parts of the Bible into braid Scots and by so doing brought fresh understanding to many.

His own understanding of human nature was warm and wide. He pretended to be cynical about it, but no one was fooled. He wrote a verse:

> The Church of Scotland is a place
> Fairly full of life,
> Where you'll find the Scottish working man
> Represented by his wife.

But he didn't leave it at that. In his parish of Cartsburn in Greenock he laboured, as he put it himself, to get father interested. 'There's no use mother flyting at the family on a Sunday morning to get out to Church,' he said, 'if the old man's lying in bed reading the *News of the World.*'

And by various means Jimmy Dow succeeded in his labours. He mixed with the men at the shipyards and in the pubs. Though he made no boast about it – in fact, he never mentioned it at all to me – he helped old ladies to paint and redecorate their houses and old men to dig their allotments. By exercising the humanity within himself he brought out the humanity in others.

One Hogmanay, in Achnamara, Jean and I had with us friends and members of the family, waiting to bring in the New Year. The hands of the clock eased towards midnight and I got up to pour out the celebration drinks. Jimmy Dow was speaking on the television. As I uncorked the first bottle his voice boomed out at me: 'And now, as the time approaches, and the man of the house has begun to fill the glasses . . .' He knew exactly what went on, did Jimmy Dow.

He died in harness, as the minister of Lochranza on the Isle of Arran. Like Willie Barclay he was never averse to a drink or a smoke. But his weaknesses were human. When he or Willie Barclay spoke or wrote, evil was stifled. And like St Paul and St Columba they purveyed Christianity not as a high-falutin' concept for saints and scholars but in terms of ordinary, everyday life. As the Padre used to say, 'There are very few saints and scholars in this world but plenty of sinners. Ministers have to tune in on their length-wave.'

(Not having learnt to speak English until the age of five, the Padre was often inclined to use the Gaelic idiom and, as he said himself, to 'put the horse before the cart'. There is no doubt, also, that his humanitarian philosophy was wonderfully broad and warm as far as his parishioners and people in general were concerned. Sometimes it came unstuck in relation to his own family!)

Willie Barclay and Jimmy Dow – and the Padre, too – were ministers who gave the lie to those clichés so often repeated in Parliament and press: 'Religion and politics don't mix. Let ministers keep their noses out of politics.'

By politics I do not mean party politics. 'Party' has now become a nasty five-letter word meaning the pursuit of personal power and financial advantage. It contains no hint of feeling for the moral welfare of the people. Politics, in my understanding, means what it infers in all the dictionaries: the study of how a nation's well-being can best be managed. One of the reasons why I hated political economy was that so many of its exponents seemed to forget that the good life has not only a material but also a spiritual side to it. The Socialists, the Tories *et al* seem to forget it, too, and almost always

Main Street, Campbeltown, *c.* 1900

The Campbeltown and Machrihanish Light Railway. Train stands in Hall Street, the Campbeltown terminus, *c.* 1920

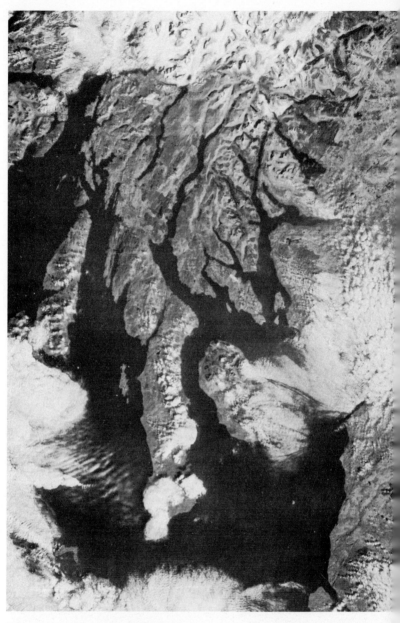

'O wad some Pow'r the giftie gie us
To see oursels as others see us!'

Southend and the Mull of Kintyre from 600 miles up

Southend Village, in the days of paraffin lamps

Iona, 1925. Funeral of Ina, Dowager Duchess of Argyll. The Padre leads the
mourners to the graveside

The Padre and 'Grannie' doing a spot of gardening

University Days. MacVicar back row, third from left. On his left, Kenneth Tyson. Seated, front right, James Davidson

Old Hugh. 'Why should I be feart?'

Kathleen Garscadden, of BBC Scottish Children's Hour with Jock, 1952

'She insisted on an ethic'

Interior of Southend Parish Church. The Padre preached from the pulpit for forty-seven years

A rare snowfall at the Mull of Kintyre. The bungalow on right is Achnamara Keil Hotel in background

Dunaverty Players in 'The Man Who Wouldn't Go to Heaven'. They went to the SCDA Western Divisional Final instead!

...cottish authors at a reception given for them by the Hutchinson Publishing ...roup in Glasgow, 1965. (*From the left*) *Back row:* Ken Gallacher, Bill ...nox, Hugh Taylor, John Quigley, Mary Faid, Archie Hind, Albert Mackie, ...ck House, Keith Middlemas, Hugh McCutcheon. *Front row:* Angus ...lacVicar, W. Murdoch Duncan, George B. Mair, Clifford Hanley, William ...errilees, Hugh MacDiarmid

'Insufferable', the author having just scored a 66 on Dunaverty Golf Course

base their propaganda on monetary considerations. What about morality?

This is where religion has a duty to interfere in politics. It can transcend the narrow party spirit and offer judgements for the good of the people in general. Politics without a religious content leads directly to hard as iron communism or fascism, in both of which love and respect for the individual is stifled and killed.

Almost two thousand years ago something apposite to the subject was said by a man who died for love: 'He that is not with me is against me.'

'The Church should never dabble in politics.' How often do we read such a statement in a newspaper leader when the General Assembly of the Church of Scotland takes a stand on some political controversy. But, of course, this kind of talk has been going on for centuries, beginning with Pontius Pilate and going on right through the Inquisition to Hitler and Stalin.

It occurred when John Knox advocated a school in every parish, because the landowners and the rich merchants were afraid that educated servants might demand higher wages. It occurred when a few compassionate ministers dared to criticize the Highland Clearances, because this made it more difficult for the lairds to clear the land of people and make room for sheep. It occurs today when the Church stands up for the oppressed and inarticulate masses in Africa, South America, Asia and elsewhere. And for why? – as we journalists are in the habit of putting it. In most cases it is because when moral values are allowed to rear disturbing heads some profit-hungry men in some profit-hungry rackets are liable to lose money.

Four hundred years ago, before John Knox, feudalism from England was spreading into the Lowlands of Scotland. Ordinary folk were beginning to be looked upon as mere chattels, born to slave for their masters. Wasn't it a good thing, in the circumstances, that the abbey monks of the time were willing to poke their noses into politics and do their best to care for and educate the people?

Those monks suffered for their interference. Some of the

abbeys were destroyed. They themselves were sometimes banished into exile. But they thought it all worth while. They refused to compromise their moral standards by knuckling down to political pressure.

Fifty years ago, having been elected to the County Council of Argyll, the Padre advocated the building of new subsidized houses for farm-workers. This, of course, was contrary to the 'politics' of having tied cottages. As a result he had to face a barrage of opposition which might have broken the spirit of a less determined character. Nowadays, in Southend, there are scores of new 'agricultural' houses. Tied cottages, as such, no longer exist, evidence that religion and politics can – and do – mix.

At the present time, industrial chaplains visit the coalfields, the shipyards and the troubled steel-works. Parish ministers go tramping through mucky village lanes and the 'deserts with windows' of the urban housing estates. When they try to point out that those who benefit from the welfare state have a moral obligation to offer something in return and give an honest day's work for an honest day's pay, they are told to keep out of politics and mind their own business.

But life as a whole, which includes men's thoughts and aspirations as well as their moral and physical health, *is* a minister's business. It is the Church's business. An individual's life cannot be divided into compartments, the Church on Sunday, politics on Monday, business on Tuesday, sport on Wednesday. Such activities are all interrelated, one influencing the other, and the end product is the character of a man.

I am sure that religion and politics cannot possibly be kept apart. Nor can either be kept apart from business or housework or sport or music or art or any other kind of human diligence. As both Willie Barclay and Jimmy Dow were often in the habit of saying: 'For what shall it profit a man, if he shall gain the whole world, and lose his own soul.'

For me they were good ministers. In some measure, small or great, they still influence what I write.

Two of my best friends in the divinity hall were Ken Tyson

and Jimmy Davidson. Ken's tall angularity and his expression, when unsmiling, of grim righteousness concealed a warm and sensitive heart. Jimmy was a small, round man who liked to smell the flowers but was often averse to the hard work of cultivation. I liked to believe that my presence was the catalyst which brought together two such contrasting characters.

I learned to admire them both and to profit from their example of unselfishness, an unselfishness which gave them a common denominator and, at times, made me feel ashamed of my own bouts of egotism. When I committed a sin Ken would lecture me, often at great length, but he would not waver at all in friendship. Jimmy would shake his head and regard me with disappointed eyes, like my mother's; but his friendship, too, was never in question.

By a coincidence, Ken served during World War II as a chaplain with the battalion of Argylls commanded eventually by my old school mate, 'Boskers' (Lt. Col. Hamish Taylor), who came to love and respect him as much as I did. Characteristically, in battle, Ken never lurked behind the troops whose spiritual welfare was his responsibility. He went forward with them, and, in the end, was wounded with them. His hurt was so severe that he never fully recovered; but physical weakness made no difference to the efforts he made to advance Christ's kingdom. First in Switzerland, then in Portugal, he ministered to congregations of Presbyterians.

When Celtic won the European Cup in 1967, Ken's manse in Lisbon was besieged after the game by supporters from Scotland who had lost their way or their money or both. That most of them were Roman Catholics mattered nothing to Ken or to his wife Renée. Their spacious grounds and most of the rooms in their manse were put at the disposal of the unexpected visitors. Fortunately it was early summer, and the Portuguese night was warm and fragrant.

Ken made and distributed scores of sandwiches and Renée made and poured out gallons of tea. Blankets were collected from members of the congregation and the stragglers made as comfortable as possible. In the morning Ken saw the British consul and, by one means or another, the Celtic supporters were sent home, subdued but still rejoicing.

And they didn't forget the kind minister and his wife in Lisbon. In due course loans were repaid in full and gifts and letters of thanks filled the manse mail-bag. 'That night,' Ken told me, 'some of the language was what you might call spicey. But I've heard worse in a board-room. As for hooliganism, not a trace of it.' But of course Ken and Renée had treated their guests like human beings, not as specimens for sociological study, and the compliment was returned.

Jimmy Davidson failed most of his divinity exams. His dreamy nature was not attuned to the idea of hard work. And he was accident prone. On one occasion I persuaded the Padre to bring him to Southend to preach. In the middle of the Lord's Prayer he developed a tickle in his throat, followed by violent spasms of coughing which caused him to bring the service to an abrupt end, lacking even a benediction. ('Poor boy!' said the Padre to me, afterwards. 'Why on earth did you bring him?') But when engaged in quiet conversation concerning history or philosophy there was never any coughing.

This friend to whom physical exercise was anathema, who would vanish from a scene of anger or mayhem like a wraith, whose pacifism remained deep and sincere, was yet a volunteer at the very beginning of World War II. He became a radio operator on a cargo ship, which, early in the war, was sunk during a German submarine attack on an Atlantic convoy. Jimmy was not listed among the survivors. His body vanished in the cold sea; but who can assert that his gentle spirit ceased to exist? In my crowded mind it still lives on, often controlling the selfish impulses invading it.

In a way, I suppose, it was selfishness which, at the end of my one and only year in divinity, prompted me to grasp the nettle and announce to all and sundry – including the Padre and my mother – that the ministry was not for me. There were other factors, of course.

There was the nagging sense that I hadn't 'received a call', that my worldly and somewhat self-seeking character was not that of a true 'Lord's servant'. There was a handicap of a stammer and the memory of an hour in a Glasgow east end church when I had stuttered and spluttered my way through a service and my friend and fellow divine, David Elder – who had arranged for me to preach there – had looked on me with pity. (I have described the horrific sequence of events in *Salt in My Porridge*. No need, therefore, to describe them again. Chills creep along my spine even now, thinking about them.)

There was also the triumph at the year's end when at last I put a metaphorical foot on the neck of political economy, passed my degree exam in the subject and, in June, 1930, was capped Master of Arts. This gave me a feeling of independence and the courage to approach the Padre with the truth.

But perhaps the most important factor behind the decision – apart from selfishness, that is – was the comparative success of my freelance writing during the year.

In January *Vain Words* had been published in *Chambers's Journal* – there it lay in the window of a stationers' shop in Great Western Road, with my name printed on the cover – and I had received the cheque for five guineas. Another short story submitted to the editor had also been accepted. The *Evening Citizen* was publishing almost everything I wrote on country matters, and the *Daily Record* was running a series of 250-word 'shorts' based on Celtic legends which, as a child, I had heard around the fireside from my parents and Maimie. And now, towards the end of my time at the university, I had won the *Daily Express* short story competition.

The cheque from Chambers's had a printed endorsement indicating that it was payment for copyright in the story. My various well-thumbed books on the writing game had all warned me that to sell copyright was the act of an idiot. The advice given was that for a normal payment – such as two guineas a thousand words – the writer of an article, short story or serial should trade to an editor only the first British serial rights – fbsr, for short. Otherwise he would be depriving himself of any claim to second British serial rights, foreign rights, broadcasting rights and all the other rights inherent in any original piece of writing. These would belong to the newspaper or magazine which had purchased the copyright in his story.

I was upset by this turn of events and, after some anxious thought, wrote a letter about it to the contemporary Scots writer whom I considered not only the best craftsman but also the most professional in the business. He was George Blake, whose popular 'Clydeside' novels I had read with admiration – and not a little envy – and who contributed regular articles and serials to the new *Scottish Daily Express*. With characteristic generosity he invited me to come and see him at a hotel. There, over his gin and tonic and my pint of draught, he dispensed wisdom, both artistic and practical, to a young writer with heather in his ears.

He described the endorsement on my cheque as an iniquitous con-trick. 'Strike it out, then put your signature on the back of the cheque in the usual way. The bank will cash it and Chambers won't argue, because in law they haven't a leg to stand on.'

I did as he advised and heard nothing more. *Vain Words* has been republished twice since then and payment for second British serial rights came to me, not to Chambers.

Later, however, there occurred an odd sequel. A subsequent story of mine published in *Chambers's Journal* before World War II was called *MacDonald's Lament*. While I was serving my king and country in various battlefields around the world – between 1940 and 1945 – *MacDonald's Lament* appeared in the *Scottish Daily Express* under another's name and without my permission. In a letter I put the facts and a strong complaint to the editor of the *Express*. Wisely, however, Sandy Trotter made no comment, and at the time I had neither the money nor the nerve to sue him (and/or Chambers) for breach of copyright.

George Blake was a short, stout man with a fighter's jaw. Physically I towered above him; but, like Brigadier Gerard facing Napoleon, I recognized my mental superior. He told me never to force my story characters into prefabricated plots. 'Let the plots develop naturally from the actions of your characters,' he said. And, always the professional, he bade me *au revoir* with this advice: 'When I write an article for a newspaper I only take a nominal fee – say, three guineas. But I claim substantial expenses, maybe as much as twenty guineas. You see, Angus, expenses are not taxable.'

Another writer who helped me was Neil Munro, whose work ranged from short stories like 'The Lost Pibroch' and novels like *The New Road* to journalism for the *Glasgow Evening News* and the brilliantly funny Para Handy books, the latter published under the pseudonym of Hugh Foulis. Like Blake, he advised me to concentrate on character. 'Study the old Highland tales told by a winter's fire,' he wrote. 'Study the flow and rhythms of our language. Study most of all the strange cantrips of the human heart.'

Both men had strong opinions on literary style.

Blake's own character was direct and down-to-earth. In his view style was an unconscious growth, created out of a writer's own personality. 'In a way,' he said, 'it's a gift. But if you keep on writing day and daily, you will find that the proper balance and rhythm of a sentence becomes instinctive. But it's the content of what you write that matters most. Why attempt to produce exquisite, polished prose if you have nothing valuable or interesting to say? Let style, my boy, take care of itself.'

Munro's 'The Lost Pibroch' is written in a distinguished style which echoes the constructions and cadences of the Gaelic language. A little to my surprise, therefore, he, also, was insistent that the matter of a story deserves more attention than the manner of its telling. He explained that in the case of 'The Lost Pibroch' he had used a particular style to harmonize with the content, which has its origins in the Gaelic character.

In youthful ignorance I voiced a fear that pressurized, written-to-a-deadline journalism might be bad for a novelist's style. Gently he demurred, though he admitted that to a great extent it depended upon the personality of the journalist. A good professional journalist, like a good professional footballer, he said, will have a style which can survive all pressures.

He himself was an example of this. His successors in Scotland today include, amongst many others, Lavinia Derwent,

Maurice Lindsay, Jack House, Alastair Phillips, Anne Simpson, Jack Webster, William Hunter, Don Whyte – and, on the sporting side, my own son Jock – all of whose work I can recognize at once, even though left unsigned. The hard work and discipline which goes to the making of a good journalist never does harm to style. The same applies to a good professional footballer, like, for example, Danny McGrain.

For my own part, I would suggest to all beginning writers that for the foundation of a literary style there is no better model than the Bible. Here the merit of simplicity in writing is revealed again and again in the stories of the Old Testament and in the Parables of the New.

The thirteenth chapter of I Corinthians (in the Authorized Version) is, for me, the ultimate example of good style. The surge and flow of its language makes a perfect vehicle for the message it contains. ('And now abideth faith, hope, charity, these three; but the greatest of these is charity.') There is a legend that the translator of this noble chapter was none other than Will Shakespeare himself. If the legend became true history, then it would not surprise me.

As for the value of simplicity in style, here is an example.

In her novel, *Barabbas*, Marie Corelli writes: 'Water having been brought, Pilate slowly lowered his hands and dipped them in the shining bowl, rinsing them over and over again in the clear, cold element, which sparkled in its polished receptacle like an opal against the fire.'

The Bible says: 'Pilate took water, and washed his hands.'

I was grateful to both George Blake and to Neil Munro for their stimulating advice. Remembering their kindness in the midst of busy lives, I try to do for beginning writers what the old professionals in my younger days did for me. Indeed, this book is being written partly for that reason, though I reckon a book by either Blake or Munro on the same subject would have been much more valuable.

I have always attempted, as they advised, to keep my style simple; but I wish I had paid more heed to their words regarding the importance of character. I was confused, however, by the insistence of some magazine editors – and of the authors of many 'practical' text-books – that the main ingredient of a good story must be the plot. I wanted so much to sell my stories – and by this means to become important in the eyes of Jean and my family and neighbours – that I concentrated on inventing ingenious plots and then making my characters conform. I was wrong, of course. Like the Padre in his form of speech, I was putting the cart before the horse. And though, through the years, my stories have been successful enough commercially, because of this many of them lack the quality I tried so hard to attain.

One of the best stories I ever wrote, in my own opinion, is *The Canisbay Conspiracy*. It came into being out of my admiration for a certain Highland lady, an aristocrat whose belief in Christian democracy and contempt for any kind of racialism were deep and strong. I let her call the tune and, in the end, found reviewers praising my 'ingenious plot'.

6. Freelance

After being capped – after putting political economy and the study of theology behind me – I returned to the Manse and announced that I was going to be a freelance writer. For my bed and board I happily contracted to pay my mother a pound a week. On my insistence, not hers.

The Padre was sceptical about my prospects. But I had shown him evidence of my industry and ability in the form of several articles and short stories which had been published, and he seemed willing enough, as he phrased it himself, to let me make 'a kirk or a mill of it'. My mother, I know, was sceptical, too, but she tried to conceal it. 'If there's a week when you can't pay – well, never mind, Angus. After all, this is your home, not a lodging house.'

But I was determined to pay and, by so doing, establish some independence.

Without the grants and bursaries I had been lucky enough to have at the university, I found, however, that to earn even a weekly pound was difficult.

That summer and autumn, when not training for or competing at the usual round of Highland Games, I laboured to produce a stream of contributions, sending them off hopefully to addresses culled from *The Writers' and Artists' Year Book*, each accompanied by the statutory stamped addressed envelope. I reckon about a quarter of them were accepted. The others came back in a tide so steady that my mother began to intercept the post and let me have my self-addressed mail only when a cheque or acceptance letter had raised my spirits. (Not until long afterwards did I learn of this, from my mother herself. 'It was the only way I thought I could help you,' she said. 'You used to look so sad when you saw your own handwriting on an envelope.')

Until now all my contributions had been handwritten. I decided that this was a possible reason why so many articles and stories came back and that, in any case, it was time that as a professional I owned a typewriter.

I went to see Angus McInnes ('Wireless and Bicycles – Repairs') in his small shop of all trades in Campbeltown. Angus was middle-aged, dark, thin as a hazel branch, with a saturnine frown which concealed a kind and utterly honest nature. A typewriter? Yes, he had a catalogue. He would send at once for the machine of my choice.

I chose a Royal Portable, price £15. Could I pay for it in instalments – instalments, say, of five shillings a week? His frown became terrible, but – yes, that could be arranged. He would let me know as soon as the typewriter arrived.

About a fortnight later Hughie Smith, the grocer from Campbeltown, made his regular weekly call at the Manse with his new motor van. He had a message for me. 'Angus McInnes wants to see you at once. You're to be prepared for bad news.'

What on earth had happened?

The next day the Padre was going to a Presbytery meeting in Campbeltown and being taken there by his elder, Jamie Hunter, one of the few people in Southend who, at the time, owned a car. I arranged to go with them. While my father and Jamie proceeded to deliberate on matters spiritual, I went to the wee shop in Longrow, troubled by matters material.

Angus saw me come in. With a look of dark evil he went to a shelf, brought down a Royal Portable in a shiny new case and laid it on the counter. 'I have played you false,' he said.

I muttered something like, 'How do you mean?'

'I told you the price was £15 and that you could pay for it at five shillings a week. I was wrong. By instalments it costs £17.' His face had become so contorted that he looked like a villain in a Pearl White film serial. 'You have every right,' he said, 'to refuse to take it.'

He meant it, too.

'Don't worry,' I said. I handed him a pound note. 'Here's

enough for the first month. I'll pay you weekly after that.'

For the first time a sort of smile softened the dark seams on his cheeks. 'I didn't want to cheat you,' he said.

Angus McInnes would have been shocked by the small print which appears in some modern contracts.

In the next ten years I rattled out an average of five thousand words a week on that typewriter, while Angus kept it in good repair. After World War II I bought another from him, and the old one went into semi-retirement. It provided amusement for Jock, when he was small, and for various inquisitive nieces and nephews. Now it has to endure assaults from the numerous grand-nieces and grand-nephews who visit us. It is badly in need of attention, I'm afraid; but Angus is no longer around to look after it, in that undeviatingly honest way of his.

To my disappointment the acquisition of a typewriter made little difference to the amount of work that was accepted, though it did, I think, help me to gain a footing with the *Bulletin*, the picture paper published by the Outram Press as companion to the *Glasgow Herald*.

The *Bulletin* was a bright publication which appealed particularly to women. Why it was killed stone dead in 1960 is a secret known only, I suppose, to the hard-faced businessmen who streamline and amalgamate. Before the war it used to run 150-words shorts called 'Little Bulletins' and a daily column under the heading of 'Pertinent and Otherwise'. The latter was composed of small items of innocuous 'society' gossip (completely unrelated to the modern William Hickey scandals in the *Daily Express*) and of 'smart' little paragraphs not unlike the 'fillers' that used to appear in *Punch*. ('A forward named Crum has been signed by lowly placed Celtic. A crumb of comfort?') For some reason I acquired the knack of writing such paragraphs and also of producing 'Little Bulletins' on subjects like ploughing matches and agricultural shows. For a 'smart' paragraph appearing in 'Pertinent and Otherwise' I was paid half a crown, by postal order; for a 'Little Bulletin' anything up to ten shillings.

But as the months slipped by into early winter and prize-money from the Highland Games was no longer available, I began to find it almost impossible to pay my mother her weekly pound and Angus McInnes his weekly five shillings. The more work I did at the typewriter the more numerous became the rejection slips. My only comfort was a statement made by Michael Joseph in *Short Story Writing for Profit* that in the first three years of his literary career, W. L. George had collected 723 of them.

I think writing is like golf. Success in both requires relaxation and a quiet mind. The harder you try to force your shots or your ideas the less worthy they turn out to be. When you are a beginning writer or a beginning golfer, however, struggling for recognition, relaxation and a quiet mind are conditions almost impossible to achieve. It is a 'Catch 22' situation.

As the winter of 1930 made a chilly passage towards spring, my acne got better; but I developed a swelling on the back of my neck, which the doctor said was an inflamed gland. If it didn't subside of its own accord, he told me, there would have to be an operation.

I wrote and typed, constantly touching and fingering the swelling to discover if it was going down. The markets I had cultivated over the past two years seemed to become less accessible, and the number of my acceptances gradually declined. I failed to understand that desperation was lowering the quality of what I wrote.

I became depressed. If it hadn't been for Jean and my mother, neither of whom ever seemed to doubt that eventually I should succeed as a writer, I think I might have joined the Foreign Legion – or done something equally eccentric – as a dramatic gesture in defiance of the world.

What made things worse was that though I often worked for twelve hours a day, some people in Southend thought I was merely being idle, dodging a proper job. Work to them meant manual labour. The idea that stringing a thousand words together to form an artistic pattern might be as tiring as ploughing a ten-acre field did not occur to them.

Along the side road to Brunerican there is a cottage called Inishrael. Today it has been made into a modern holiday home by our close friends, Roddy and Marjorie McSween. At that time it was an ordinary greystone cottage, enclosed by byres and loose-boxes, and occupied by an elderly spinster whose name was Janet McCaig. Her only companion was a collie dog, ill-tempered and slightly deranged like his mistress. I remember passing the cottage one night, on my way home from seeing Jean. There at the gate stood the collie, barking and baring his teeth at me. And there at the door stood Janet, shouting obscenities. 'Away and work, you lazy runt! Away and work!'

I tried to ignore them both. As the barking and the shouting died away behind me I thought of all the hard work I had done, with small success and much failure at the end of it. I thought of Jean, with the prospect of marriage and a home of our own like an unseen oasis across a desert of poverty. I thought of my parents and my family, all disappointed and losing respect for me. I thought of my gland, still hard and sore and cringed at the knowledge that soon I should have to spend time in the Campbeltown Cottage Hospital having it doctored. There in the dusk, along the river-side, alone except for a few cows in the Inishrael meadow, I sat down on a stone. I let a tide of Hebridean gloom and self-pity flood over me. I cried.

But life went on. The gland was operated on successfully, and during my convalescence euphoria returned. I decided I was going to write a novel.

Janet McCaig had not always been considered 'a borderline case'. For years her brother Archie had been with her, guiding her actions and imposing discipline when required. When he died, between the wars, it gradually became clear how devotedly he had looked after his sister, concealing from us the true extent of her mental imbalance.

Archie McCaig was one of my father's elders, a small, square, grey-bearded man with a stiff neck, the result of rheumatism. He had a quick sense of humour, and a gift for storytelling. When I was in my early teens I used to accompany the Padre on all his 'visitations' to Inishrael, so that I could listen to Archie's talk.

The first inkling I got that Janet might be 'peculiar' was after he had entertained the Padre and me with one of his most exciting yarns. It concerned a fishing expedition off the Mull of Kintyre arranged by himself and two members of the McEachran family, Colin and Hugh. The boat belonged to the McEachrans and, indeed, had been built by them; and it may have been fortunate that it was a stout, homemade craft, because on that particular evening, on the way home, it was overtaken by a storm before it could reach the shelter of the slip at Dunaverty.

Archie's description of the storm and of their efforts to fight it made me thrill with admiration. I was there in the boat with them, the cold sea lifting and breaking around me, the spray stinging my eyes, the sweat tangling my hair as I rowed with the burly McEachrans and Archie, at the tiller, kept his eyes on the distant slip.

'We were being tossed about something terrible. I could see Colin McEachran was getting tired – he was about fifty at the time – and though Hugh, being younger, was still pulling hard, the tide was beginning to turn against us. "What do you think, boys," I said, "a wee rest and a bit of a prayer?" The McEachrans nodded and leant forward on their oars. They were needing all their breath, so I took it on myself to say the prayer.'

My father said: 'What prayer, Archie?'

'Well, I gave them the Lord's Prayer, minister, and the storm was so loud I had to shout it. Then I got the McEachrans to sing the verse of a psalm with me. "Yea, though I walk in death's dark vale . . ." '

'What happened then?' I said.

'It was a strange thing, boy, but after the prayer and the psalm the storm seemed to go down a bit and the McEachrans found new life. Just as it was getting dark we reached the slip.' He glanced at my father. 'And you know, minister, when we climbed ashore and felt the hard stone under our feet, we knelt down there by one of the bollards and said another prayer. In thanks to God.'

I sighed with satisfaction at the conclusion of a good story skilfully told. But Janet, who had been sitting in the shadows beyond the peat fire, suddenly sat forward and addressed her brother. 'Did ye get ony fush?' she inquired.

I saw that only with difficulty did the Padre keep his face straight. I followed his example.

Archie said: 'Tut, tut, Janet! That'll do!' Then he went on to speak about something else.

Left alone in Inishrael, Janet's condition deteriorated. She began shouting at people passing on the farm road and, indeed, often went across to Brunerican to bang on doors and windows and make animal sounds at those inside. Jean became terrified of her.

At one stage Janet was treated in a mental hospital, but in the years before World War II she returned to the cottage.

I was away from Southend, in the King's employ, when the end came. By all accounts it was bizarre and cruel.

One morning Jean's brother Peter, passing the cottage on his way to an outlying field, found the doors locked and barred. He peered in at the kitchen window and saw Janet stretched on the 'set-in' bed, clad in her night-clothes, with the collie lying beside her. He opened the window and tried to climb inside, but the collie, leaping, barking and snarling, kept him at a distance. He could see no motion of breathing in Janet's chest and was convinced that she was dead.

He went back to the farm and telephoned for the doctor and the police; and presently Dr Niven arrived, along with Constable John McVicar, the local policeman, and Constable Crae McIntyre, driver of the police car. But when Constable McVicar did what Peter had done and tried to enter by the kitchen window, he, too, was attacked by the dog and had to move out again, quickly.

The collie returned to the bed and stood there, barking, suspicious slavers dripping from his mouth.

Constable McVicar said to Peter: 'Have you got a gun?' Peter nodded.

So did Dr Niven. 'Seems it's the only way,' he said.

The spread of the pellets from a shot-gun was the problem. By some means the dog had to be lured away from the bed. Finally, Constable McIntyre stretched inside the window and threw a stick into a corner of the kitchen. As the collie leapt to attack it, Peter fired and, in spite of the tension, did not miss.

The doctor found that Janet had been dead for some time, perhaps since the previous night as she got into bed.

When I heard it, the story haunted me for weeks. I had hated old Janet on account of her obscene shouting and for her harassment of Jean and her brothers in Brunerican. But did any human being, however unprepossessing, deserve such a gruesome death-bed?

'There is a divinity within every man,' Professor Bowman had told us, his students. 'Respect and reverence for this divinity is the foundation of civilized behaviour.' I had agreed with him. 'Love your neighbour,' was the message of the New Testament. I had agreed with that, too. But as far as Janet McCaig was concerned I had failed to put such beautiful theories into practice, and now it was too late to do anything about it.

I was learning how difficult it is to live a life of high principle. And how guilt, once experienced, has a habit of clinging to the spirit like a burr.

I also began to learn the difference between stories based on ordinary life and the contrived products recommended by the editors of popular magazines between the wars. I was fool enough not to take the lesson to heart. I continued to equate money-making with ingenious plots in which stock characters lived and moved and had their ersatz being. I was prostituting any artistic talents I possessed in much the same way as soft-porn novelists do today. Like them, I was writing what editors and publishers told me the public wanted. I was doing what I often preached against in print: denying the spiritual content of life for the sake of a possible material benefit.

Part of my trouble may have been that as a Scot I was trying too hard to achieve an English ethos.

At that time the first underground rumblings of nationalism were being felt. Vaguely I welcomed them, because it seemed to me that the Scots – and Scots writers in particular – were at a disadvantage when it came to selling their products in London. Apparently our contributions had to be of the Harry Lauder variety before they were allowed to compete with sophisticated southern culture. By every inference we were made to feel inferior by smooth English operators who had never even heard of the Arbroath Declaration.

In the past fifty years the nationalistic rumblings have threatened to become an earthquake. In many ways I wish they hadn't, because my instinct is for union rather than for separation in all departments of life. I suppose, however, that Scottish 'rebellion' against English attitudes was bound to happen, not on a 'racist' basis but as a kind of protest against government from far away and the creeping bureaucracy which such government creates.

Some Englishmen still do not understand this. Not long ago, happily riding north, I met one on the Flying Scotsman. On first acquaintance he appeared to be a reasonable fellow, possibly a member of the CBI. But when, inadvertently, I mentioned the Scottish Assembly he snorted and exclaimed: 'Devolution! Why did it happen? Who the heck do you Scots think you are?'

'A good question,' I said.

In my best preaching style I went on to explain that we are small and dark, like the Stone Age men who came from Ireland 8000 years ago; lean and red-haired like the painted Picts; stout and strong like the Brythons and Anglo-Saxons who have always, through the ages, kept moving in from the south; tall and fair like the Norsemen who, a thousand years ago, temporarily imposed their will on part of Scotland; and finally, loud-voiced and burly like the Scotti, the Irish tribesmen who crossed the narrow sea in the first centuries AD and gave us not only St Columba but also an identity and a name.

'A lot of mongrels,' said my English friend.

I resisted a temptation to quote Darwin's observation that mongrels, as a rule, are highly intelligent. Instead I agreed that there is no such thing as a typical Scot. (Is there, for that matter, a typical Englishman?)

I said: 'An old-fashioned belief is that Highlanders are either happy and energetic or sad and lazy according to their mood; that Lowlanders and east-coasters are dour and hard-working, tight-fisted and lacking in humour. But Highlanders can be dour and Lowlanders happy, and east-coasters can be full of fun.

'Then there are the Jews,' I went on, indulging myself. 'And the Italians and the Cypriots and the Indians and the Pakistanis. They are Scots, too. Some of them wear the kilt, and one Indian I know has invented his own tartan. If you saw our Pakistani boys and girls from Lewis singing Gaelic songs at the Mod you would be charmed.'

He looked more dazed than charmed. 'And you have the supporters of Rangers and Celtic,' he sneered.

'Yes. We go to football matches and play golf, just as they do in England. We attend the opera and dig disco sessions. We are Protestants and Roman Catholics, dukes and lairds and miners and farmers and fishermen. We argue and fight among ourselves. We make love and do our good neighbour bit. We laugh at and with each other and occasionally get drunk. Sometimes we even talk amicably together – that is, when we're allowed to get a word in edgeways by such dreary publicists as Iain Sproat, Mike McGahey and Teddy Taylor.'

Sourly he said: 'So you admit things have changed since Bannockburn?'

'Of course. But the people of Scotland still think in the same way.'

'Now you're going to quote from that bloody Declaration of Arbroath?'

I was, but not the bit he expected.

'Should he, the Bruce, abandon our cause or aim at reducing us or our kingdom, we will instantly expel him as a common enemy and, under God, choose another King.'

A blank look had come into his eyes, so I continued: 'I know. It's hard to believe that such words were written in 1320, while Bruce was at the height of his power and popularity. But for me, as for most Scots, they come echoing down the years as a trumpet call for democracy.'

I had him now. Like the Ancient Mariner I pursued my advantage. 'For years we Scots have been brainwashed with the idea that no one is important except as a citizen of the country as a whole, except as a member of a union or of the CBI. Statistics and balance sheets are being offered in place of character. Big Brothers – in London and in Europe – are doing their utmost to smother individuals and communities under great blankets of bureaucracy. Now, by means of devolution, we are trying to preserve our individuality. And our small community, which, we believe, like our family life, is a main source of strength and happiness in an increasingly soul-less world.

'St Andrew and Bannockburn,' I said, 'Glencoe and the Clearances, even the "Hungry Twenties" and "the black, black oil", are only of marginal importance in our effort to slough off poverty – a poverty, I may add, which is spiritual rather than material. When the Royal Scots Fusiliers stormed ashore in Sicily, men fought and died for their regiment only incidentally for the British Army. People like St Columba and St Margaret, Wallace and Bruce, Robert Burns, Sir Walter Scott and David Livingstone have all left behind them examples of nobility, not because they were neatly documented citizens of the country as a whole but because they were independent individuals, ready to sacrifice wealth and comfort, even their very lives, to uphold the values of freedom and freedom of thought so dear to them as Scots.'

My English friend yawned. When we parted at Glasgow Central station he was shaking his head. He still didn't understand.

And while on the subject of understanding, here is something we Scots don't understand. Why is it that those Englishmen who sneer most at Scots meanness and Scots 'coarseness' and Scots poverty in thought and action – why is it that those Englishmen are the loudest in condemning devolution and separatism? If they think of us so poorly, why don't they jump at the chance of getting rid of us? Or is their thinking influenced, after all, by visionary fountains of 'the black, black oil?'

Will the English – and the quisling Scots – ever understand? Will they ever understand that, like Frank Sinatra, we want to do it our way? And make a kirk or a mill of it.

My decision to write a novel was a calculated bid for fame
and fortune. I surveyed the publishing scene and came to the
conclusion that the story most likely to become a best-seller
was an adventure story, spiced with romance. 'Sapper' had
followed the formula with success. So had Dornford Yates,
E. Charles Vivian, William Le Queux, George Birmingham,
Horace Hutchinson – and, of course, John Buchan.

Among them all John Buchan was my personal favourite,
even though most of his Scots 'heroes' had been to English
public schools and most of his 'native' Scots were underlings,
quaintly lovable characters such as poachers, forelock-
touching estate-workers and unlettered Labour MPs. His
women, too, were disappointing as far as I was concerned:
cool, supremely well-mannered maidens who gave no promise of passion among the corn-stacks and who, it seemed to
me, were put into his books merely as an acknowledgment
that another sex besides the male happened to exist. Despite
all this, however, my admiration of the stride and impetus of
his storytelling was tremendous. And still is.

On the other hand, in my novel, I proposed to make my
heroes 'native' – real Scots, living in Scotland – and my
heroines as sexy as my experience allowed. In my dreams I
outsold Buchan by many thousands of copies.

Back in the Manse after 'my operation', and with a bandage still sticky and uncomfortable around my neck, I got
down to business. In the mornings I wrote a thousand words
in a thick exercise book which I had bought for ninepence in
the *Courier* shop in Campbeltown. (A similar one, today,
costs 75p.) In the afternoons I typed them out on the Royal
Portable. For the first chapter or two I enjoyed myself, and
my mother and Jean both remarked that I looked happier
and healthier. But then, as I paused to count up all the words
I had written and found that they numbered less than
10 000, I began to realize what a long and sustained effort
was required to complete 80 000 words, which, before World
War II, was the usual length for a popular novel.

At present, partly because of printing costs, comparable
books contain only 50 000 words. This makes for a much
more tightly written and, therefore, more readable story,

especially in the case of an ordinary 'thriller'. The amount of padding that went into pre-war pot-boilers had to be read to be believed. Long descriptions of dull scenery, 'stream of consciousness' analyses of what occurred – or failed to occur – in the minds of heroes and heroines, recapitulations of the carpentered plots – all such devices held up the action and, no doubt, bored some impatient readers to the point of an immediate return of the books to the library.

For myself, I had no clear vision of what length my story ought to be. I went by what *The Writers' and Artists' Year Book* told me was the 'correct' number of words and laboured blindly towards that goal. I lashed my brain into daily action, fought hard against inherent laziness, tried to ignore my dangerously dwindling financial resources, shut out the awful prospect of the book eventually being rejected and tried to present a happy, confident face to the world.

That summer I did my usual stint at the Highland Games but without great success. So much sitting at a table, writing and typing, kept me from being fully fit, physically. In any case, my mind was elsewhere, grappling with events and characters in *The Purple Rock*.

Weeks went by. Months went by, three of them. And it was autumn. It was also nearly the end as far as my money was concerned. I could still pay the instalments on the typewriter; but my mother, during the last month, had to do without her pounds. She made no complaint.

I finished the book and counted the words. They totalled only slightly more than 60 000, still almost 20 000 less than the number advised. But I felt exhausted, incapable of starting to expand and pad. In any case, I was down to my last few shillings, and it seemed to me that the time had come to stifle feelings of pride and independence and find a job with a regular pay-packet.

Consulting my *Writers' and Artists' Year Book*, I made a short list of literary agents to whom I might entrust the selling of my book and wrote to them all, asking if they would consider handling a novel by an unknown writer. The most encouraging reply came from Miss Patience Ross of A. M.

Heath & Co., Ltd. To her I sent off the manuscript of *The Purple Rock*.

In about three weeks Miss Ross replied that she liked the book and would try to find a publisher for it. This made me jump with joy; but even so, I was too innocent and inexperienced to realize how lucky I was. Agents like Heath, with a high reputation, are often more choosey than publishers. Perhaps it was easier in those days to storm the ramparts, because the book trade was booming, even bursting at the seams. Now, in this age of inflation and high printing costs, to acquire a good agent is not easy. For the past few years, instead of expanding their lists, agents, like publishers, have been pruning them. My heart grieves for a beginning writer today. The road to publication is far steeper and more dangerous than the one, in youthful ignorance, I so blithely followed.

With the future of my book in expert hands, I went to Alec MacLeod, editor and owner of the *Campbeltown Courier*, and asked him, humbly, if by any chance he could give me a job. Here again I was lucky. 'Why not?' Alec said, shifting a peppermint from one stout cheek to another. 'I've been editor, reporter, chief sub-editor and office boy in this place far too long. I think I deserve a little peace to write things for the paper that really interest me. All right. Come as a reporter. Three pounds a week. A bonus at Christmas, and you can keep the payments for any freelance stuff you sell to outside papers.'

I was dumbfounded. I was also extremely happy. Regions of wealth were suddenly being opened up. It occurred to me, also, that many people were able to get married on £3 a week. Back at the Manse and at Brunerican, I boasted of my new status as a writer gainfully employed.

'Good!' said the Padre. 'Now you can learn your trade.'

'I always *said* you'd make a good reporter,' my mother told me.

Maimie remarked: 'Now maybe we'll get some Southend news in the *Courier!*'

Archie, at the university, Willie at sea and Rona, Kenneth and John at school were all obviously relieved that their eldest brother would no longer hang grumpily around when they were at home.

People in Southend seemed glad that, as they saw it, I had begun to work at last. I put aside the ignoble suspicion that some of those who now became ultra-friendly were hoping I might put their names in the paper. Or, perhaps, in certain circumstances, keep them out.

'Not long now,' I told Jean. 'I'll open a bank account the day I get my first pay.'

She made a fuss of me and baked a fairy-light sponge, filled with fresh whipped cream, to celebrate. We had now been 'wenching', as the neighbours called it, for more than five years. She was accustomed to my moods. This was one of triumph; but she knew there would be more of despair to come. In consequence, I don't think she shared my high optimism. She was content, however, patient creature that she was – and is – to enjoy the moment and to let the future take care of itself.

7. *Courier* Special

For almost two years I helped Alec MacLeod with the *Courier*, as I have recounted in *Salt in My Porridge*. In those two years I learned much about the writing trade and even more about human nature.

Alec also put into practice the ideas that had come to him during our interview. After a few weeks' coaching on the technical side, I was allowed to take over his former roles as reporter, sub-editor and office-boy, while he himself took life more easily and wrote a series of feature articles about local characters and customs. He took the pen-name 'Neonach', which, in the Gaelic, means 'an awkward fellow'. But there was nothing awkward about his style of writing. Like George Blake and Neil Munro, he was an advocate of simplicity. 'It's easy to use flowery language,' he often told me, echoing Sandy Banks, my old English master. 'Not so easy to be straightforward.' He agreed with J. B. Priestley that a writer ought to be able to share his thoughts and impressions with the crowd. 'Shakespeare could do it,' he would say. 'No intellectual snobbery for him.'

Another important lesson he tried to teach me was that above all else a writer must have integrity, both moral and artistic. 'Never express an opinion that you don't believe in,' he said once, smacking his lips on the peppermint that took the place of the tobacco-wad he had chewed long years before as an apprentice printer. 'You might be tempted to do so in order to please me or some other editor. I'd respect you far more if you displeased me with something I knew came from your heart. And so would any editor worth his salt. Insincerity always shows and lowers the reputation not only of the paper but also of its readers.'

To observe Alec's law, fifty years ago, was difficult. Today, it is infinitely more difficult. I know three big-name journalists in the contemporary Scottish scene who callously flout it. Two of them vote Labour but write anti-Labour articles for Tory papers. The third votes Tory but lends his name to virulent criticism of the Tories in a Labour paper. They do it for the money, which they consider more important than principle. Is there a clue here as to why so much public suspicion and lack of respect has recently been shown for the media?

Despite recurring evidence to the contrary, I believe that the great majority of our politicians, businessmen, trade unionists and writers are honourable and decent folk. The trouble is that in our day, encouraged by the media, a few mavericks in each category keep trying to hide behind the skirts of the honourable and decent by side-stepping 'integrity' and, in the process, prostituting the English language.

At one time, when a VIP was interviewed on radio or television or quoted in the press, good people were inclined to accept his or her honesty. But with the development of an amoral and even anti-Christian quality in the art of public relations, good people are becoming confused. And suspicious. One or two coins in the currency of truth have been exposed and found to be made of lead, and the genuine ones are in danger of being devalued.

After a study of the media in recent years I have compiled, for my own guidance, a small dictionary of words and phrases, the original meanings of which have become obscured.

Here are three examples from the political section, beginning with the word 'integrity' itself.

Once upon a time a noble word, '*integrity*' is now used frequently in reference to a politician who, aided by lawyers and public relations experts, has so far been able to cover his guilty tracks. (Cf. 'There will be no whitewash at the White House.')

'*I have already made it perfectly clear*.' Nearly always, in a modern context, this means 'I have already dodged the question in a bout of double-talk and intend to repeat the process.'

'*He has a brilliant intellect.*' This phrase is occasionally employed to camouflage idleness and lack of public conscience. More often, however, it is applied to a politician whose speech-writers have access to *The Oxford Dictionary of Quotations.*

From the business section:

'*I welcome the investigation.*' This can mean 'I'm afraid I have been lumbered, but with professional assistance I will do my best to fudge the issue.'

'*Resignation from the board is my only honourable course.*' A gambit used in an effort to distract attention from a course which, up to date, has been strictly dishonourable.

'*There is a lack of confidence abroad.*' In certain cases this can be translated as 'Ordinary people in our own country are receiving so large a slice of the financial cake that the enormous profits made by foreign banks and lending institutions are in danger of being eroded.'

From the trade union section:

'*I speak for the workers.*' There is a danger that this may mean, simply, 'I speak for a few communists intent upon disruption for disruption's sake.'

'*Comrades.*' Another noble word which now, in specific circumstances, implies 'Fellow Marxists – and stuff all other members of the human race.'

'*I believe in the equal distribution of wealth.*' A platitude which often boils down to 'Soak the rich – okay – but let nothing interfere with my differentials.'

From the literary section:

'*An adult play which ignores the conventions.*' Usually a play dwelling upon sex and sadism completely lacking in artistic discipline and of little interest to normal people above the age of puberty.

'*A sensitive study.*' Common description of a novel dealing with homosexuality (for sales purposes).

'*Frank, outspoken, ingenious, Scottish to the core.*' This could well be the description of a play written in an obscure Scottish dialect, interlarded with 'daring' words like 'Christ' and 'bugger' but lacking entirely in loving respect for humanity.

It seems today that a few people are more intent upon 'projecting an image' than upon being honest with themselves and their neighbours and telling the truth as they see it. Even more to blame for this than politicians, businessmen, trade unionists and writers are some of the high-powered advertising and public relations moguls, who – along with the proliferating 'financial experts' – are attempting to rule our lives.

According to certain ad-men, the sight of a new feminine 'hair-do', a manly pipe or a yachtsman's cap has more influence upon us, the so-called 'masses', than frankness and sincerity of heart. What do they take us for? Morons? I'm afraid their answer might be a cynical 'Yes'.

Standards in the use of the English language are falling. Why? It seems to me there is only one answer: 'Because moral standards are falling.' And why are moral standards falling? Because, I believe, a mob of 'clever-dicks', some seeking personal power, most of them financial profit, are working overtime, doing their utmost to undermine the value and authority of the Christian faith.

A high-water mark in this tide of exploitation was the launching some years ago of the new cult of 'punk rock'. A group of 'musicians' calling themselves the Sex Pistols, previously signed up by the recording firm of EMI for £40 000, appeared on Thames Television, in which EMI has shares. Their performance, musically, was terrible. But it was accompanied by obscene words and gestures which caused an immediate shocked reaction from viewers and sections of the press. This, of course, was what the group's management had foreseen. Free publicity burgeoned for the Sex Pistols. 'Punk rock' was on the way, its innovators intent upon the financially rewarding exercise of assaulting and raping innocent young minds.

A few wet behind the ears sociologists argued that such 'happenings' were excusable on the grounds of freedom of expression and changing standards.

Freedom of expression? Freedom cannot exist in a world of moral anarchy.

Changing standards? Nearly two thousand years ago

Christ indicated the only kind of behaviour that ensures general human happiness. He said: 'Love your neighbour.' He didn't mean – with an ad-man's snide giggle – 'Con your neighbour.' He meant, as Professor Bowman pointed out to us in the class of moral philosophy, 'Give your neighbour the reverence and respect due to him or her as another human being.'

(It seems that the 'punk rock' publicity did not build up the outstanding success anticipated by the Sex Pistols. When I spoke on the telephone to a representative of EMI, he told me that sales of their records were 'disappointing'. Perhaps we, the 'masses', are not such morons after all.)

I enjoyed my work on the *Courier*, untroubled either by PROs or by ad-men. In a small community like Kintyre everybody knows the last domestic detail about everybody else. 'Image making', therefore, has always been regarded here as a futile exercise. Untroubled also by trade union rules, I roamed the town and countryside, chatting to people and gathering 'copy', heedless of set hours. I helped Alec to read proofs and insert heads and cross heads. I helped the printers when their work-load became heavy, as it often did on a Wednesday, the day before the paper was printed. I lived in digs in Campbeltown, paying Mrs Rankin in Cross Street 22s 6d per week, and felt it no burden to rise at six in the morning to give a hand in the composing room with wedding invitations, agricultural show catalogues – and, sometimes, urgent, black-edged funeral notices – and then to work on until eight o'clock in the evening collecting copy from, for example, the Sheriff Court, the winner of a local football pool, fishermen back from a spell at the herring in Loch Fyne.

And afterwards, in a pub, perhaps to meet a character like Big Nan, sixteen burly stones of her, who drank pint for pint with the men and outdid even the quay 'lumpers' in the coarse quality of her language.

Big Nan had a boyfriend, a wee crinkled shoemaker nicknamed the Skate, who, though socially backward and silent, was yet noted for his masculine powers. (To handle Big Nan certainly required an expert.) One night, in the Diamond Vaults, the talk turned to the latest Engagements announcement in the *Courier*, that of a distillery owner's poetry writing son to a laird's daughter. Giggling gossip had it that when he proposed the young man had gone down on his knees and recited:

> 'As fair art thou, my bonnie lass,
> So deep in luve am I;
> And I will luve thee still, my dear,
> Till a' the seas gang dry.'

I turned to Big Nan. 'What would you say if the Skate got all romantic and did the same to you?'

She snorted into her tankard. 'I'd say the bugger was drunk!' she declared.

The only jobs I did not relish were interviews with relatives of people who had died and whom Alec reckoned deserved 'obits' in the paper. In a house of mourning I became awkward and uneasy, a curtain in my brain blotting out many of the questions I planned to ask. Alec knew my weakness and often wrote the obituaries himself, from personal knowledge of the deceased. 'A reporter is like a doctor,' he said to me, once. 'In the face of death he's got to harden his heart and try to think objectively.' But I noticed that, like me, he avoided as much as possible physical intrusions upon grief.

One day I went to the home of a young man in his early twenties who had been killed when his horse bolted and the cart in which he was conveying wet draff from a distillery to an outlying farm had overturned.

His older sister sat staring into the cold kitchen range. She told me her father had gone out. 'He'll get drunk. He always does.'

'May I speak to your mother?'

'She's in there. In the back room.'

I opened the door of the small bedroom. I saw the corpse on the bed. The mother lay across it, weeping. She had cancer in one breast. Her blouse was open and the bandage on her breast had slipped. I saw pale red flesh. Pus was oozing out of it on to the corpse.

I shut the door and went through the kitchen to the back yard, where I retched up my dinner.

When I told Alec, he said: 'For some folks, Angus, life is no joke.'

I wanted it to be a joke. I still feel that it ought to be a joke, though sometimes the humour may have a black edge to it.

Having to write about five thousand words every week for a small provincial paper like the *Campbeltown Courier*, I learned the basic principle of journalism: *Names make news*. A long list of prize-winners at a bird show was more viable 'copy' than a poetic piece about a sunset. A report on, for example, the annual 'Kiltie Ball' had no relevance unless it bristled with the names of the high-ranking officers and their women-folk who sat at the top table and those of the corporals and privates who manned the door and the bar.

For a reporter, such attention to detail was more important during my time on the *Courier* than it is today, when photographs can be produced straight away from a glossy print. Fifty years ago, if we wanted a picture in the paper, we had to send the print to a firm in Glasgow which specialized in block-making. The result was that news pictures were seldom available to us in time, and names which should have appeared in captions had to be included in long swatches of copy.

Another lesson I learnt was how to write at speed against a deadline.

I remember a sheep-stealing case which ended in the Sheriff Court late on a Wednesday evening. By six o'clock on a Wednesday, as a rule, almost every scrap of copy was set and ready in the flat-bed machine so that a quick start could be made the following morning. Alec was willing to print the verdict only and hold over until the next issue a detailed report of the final day's proceedings; but I insisted on remaining in the office until midnight to complete it. Then I persuaded Archie MacMillan, the linotype operator, to come in early the next morning to set it up. Archie was as keen as I to show off his professional skill, and we were both proud peacocks when, before lunch time on Thursday, the paper was on the streets, with posters announcing: '*Sheep-stealing Trial – Full Report*'.

Though always sparing of praise – a common characteristic of editors – Alec was pleased about it. For once we had 'scooped' our prestigious rival, the *Oban Times*.

Not long after I joined the paper Alec MacLeod's wife took ill and he came less eagerly to the office. I found myself more and more involved in the intricate details of producing a paper each Thursday. In my secret thoughts I fancied myself as a whizz-kid editor and specialized in what at the time – under the influence of American films – were called 'scoops': in my case stories of local interest which I reckoned had been overlooked by the *Oban Times* or by the other Campbeltown paper, the *Argyllshire Herald*. Gleefully I printed them under headings in large black type: *COURIER SPECIAL*. In this ploy I had an advantage, because the *Courier* came out a day earlier than the *Oban Times* and *Herald*.

Big Sandy McMurchy, Arthur Henderson and Archie MacMillan – the entire printing staff – were all dubious about such revolutionary antics on the part of the conservative *Courier*. 'Alec wadna like it,' I was told. But the game was exciting – and I think that in a way they enjoyed hearing the *Courier* being talked about in the town – so, as long as Alec remained absent, they played along with me.

I kept asking in the office if the sales of the *Courier* were going up; but it seemed that in spite of all my brilliant efforts they remained much the same as they had done during the past fifty years. It was disappointing news for a whizz-kid whose joy in life depended so much upon competition.

Why compete at all if no tangible prize is forthcoming at the end of the day? During my term of employment with the *Courier* I discovered a personal answer. For me, competition for its own sake is enjoyable. Prizes, in a material sense, are irrelevant. I believe all writers who aim to endure must possess this philosophy. Almost certainly they will not gain large monetary prizes. But the more valuable prizes of inner satisfaction and independence are theirs for the taking.

Alec MacLeod's wife died. A week later he came back to the office, sad and even tearful, but determined to find comfort in work. He never discussed the *COURIER SPECIALS* with me, but they quickly disappeared, and the paper settled back into its former groove of solid worth. Advertising shopkeepers no longer complained that the paper was boosting brash new rivals at their expense. Town councillors no longer invaded the office to accuse me of giving more prominence to a colleague's 'smart alec' speeches than to their own more pedestrian but more 'sensible' ones. Members of the Presbytery of Kintyre – including the Padre – were relieved that reports of their meetings no longer highlighted the social scandals to which they sometimes referred, almost apologetically, but concentrated instead on the unctious utterings of establishment divines.

But Alec allowed me still to have my way with the 'Sparks and Flashes' column. I had made a number of good friends among the agricultural community who were always willing to supply me with the latest humorous gossip at some fellow farmer's expense – that is, as long as I promised not to divulge the source of my information. Provided that the jokes were good-natured and hurtful to nobody, I embellished them and printed them in black type, much to our country readers' delight – even sometimes to the delight of the victim.

One of my most prolific informants, as I can now reveal, was Willie Smith, a bachelor farmer whose gusty laughter often used to fill the office on a Monday morning. (Monday was – and still is – market day in Campbeltown.) But Willie had a terrible come-uppance. At the autumn show of the Kintyre Agricultural Society a small sensation occurred when, competing with hordes of expert ladies, Willie carried off the first prize in the bramble jam section. This was nothing, however, to the sensation caused by a paragraph in the following week's 'Sparks and Flashes' which revealed that Willie's jam was, in fact, bramble jelly into which, at the semi-liquid stage, whole brambles had been cunningly inserted.

'Who the hell tellt ye that?' thundered Willie, when I met him on the street.

'You'd be surprised,' I said.

'It's a bloody liberty!'

'But true?'

He burst out laughing. 'Ay, it's true. But I ken bloody fine who gi'ed the show away. Here, let me tell ye somethin' aboot him ...'

I made some good friends among the fishermen, too. In those days, the early thirties, farmers led anxious and impoverished lives, with milk selling at only 3½p per gallon. Fishermen found existence equally hard. The behaviour of the herring shoals had become less predictable; and, in any case, the herring was losing its popularity as part of a fashionable diet.

One sea-faring friend I made was Duncan Newlands, who later became coxswain of the Campbeltown life-boat. His most famous rescue was that of fifty-four passengers and crew of the American liberty ship, *Byron Darnton*, wrecked on Sanda in March 1946. He worked at various jobs – line-fishing, boat hiring, 'quay lumping'. I remember him talking to me indignantly about the slump in the herring trade. 'Why people turn up their noses at a wholesome fresh herring beats me! I expect if you put out a story that herrings were a rare delicacy – like caviare, which in some countries is as common as porridge – you'd get folk fighting to buy them!'

An old man, now retired, Duncan has seen his flight of imagination become reality. In his younger days, when herrings were sold at threepence a dozen, only the very poor were inclined to buy them. Now, when they cost about 20p each, well-heeled housewives queue up to add them to their fashionable menus.

' *"I am ruminating,"* said Mr Pickwick, *"on the strange mutability of human affairs."*

' *"Oh! I see – in at the palace door one day, out at the window the next. Philosopher, sir?"*

' *"An observer of human nature, sir,"* said Mr Pickwick.'

Duncan did most of his fishing at night. By day he often used his boat – the *Orange Blossom* – to go out and meet the

'puffers', thus making certain that he secured a job, unload-
ing coal.

The puffers used to come to Campbeltown bringing house
and industrial coal – industrial coal mainly for the distilleries
– from the Ayrshire pits. They tied up at the Old Quay and
were unloaded by means of iron buckets winched up out of
the holds and then emptied directly into horse-drawn carts
and lorries. And into waggons belonging to the Campbeltown and Machrihanish Light Railway. Several men were
always needed in the holds to fill the buckets.

This was the kind of work eagerly sought by Duncan, and
it was a recognized thing that the first man to board an
incoming puffer got the bucket-filling jobs. When a puffer
was due in the harbour all types of craft would sail out to
meet her, and often, in the end, it would develop into a race.
'I've seen me, with my mates,' Duncan once told me, 'going
as far as Ayr harbour, nearly forty miles away, to contact a
puffer and "put our line aboard", as we called it.'

When regattas were held in Campbeltown, between the
wars, races inspired by this idea were arranged for the 'quay
lumpers', the competing punts being propelled by shovels
instead of oars.

In the scramble for jobs, the *Orange Blossom*, which had
an engine, gave Duncan an advantage over his oar-bound
rivals. At the end of it all, however, pay for filling the buckets amounted to less than 2½d per ton. But with shipbuild-
ing no longer viable in Campbeltown, with the town's distilleries closing down one after another, with the low price of
milk, butter and cheese making paupers out of farmers and
with the herring disappearing not only from the usual
fishing-grounds but also from the nation's frying-pans, work
was tragically scarce in Kintyre. People like Duncan who
could find jobs of any kind, no matter how poorly paid, were
the lucky ones. Those who didn't had to beg for a pitiful
dole, amounting in some cases to only a few shillings a week.

While I worked on the *Courier* the national unemployment figure was well over two million. Marketing boards and
the resultant bureaucracy, militant trade unions and the
resultant aggro became inevitable.

Meanwhile, on 28 October 1932, my twenty-fourth birth-day, a cruising seagull dropped a slimy 'message' on my head. 'Sign o' good luck!' said Duncan, with whom I was talking at the time. How right he was. Later in the day a letter arrived from A. M. Heath & Co. Ltd. Miss Patience Ross was 'happy to tell me' that my book, *The Purple Rock*, had been accepted for publication by Stanley Paul.

8. Rocks in My Porridge

For days after the acceptance of *The Purple Rock* I was insufferable to Jean and my family. Success always goes to my head. My neighbour, Allan Lamont, once introduced me to a golfing opponent as 'the best and most graceful loser in the business but the most obnoxious winner you're ever likely to meet.' I made a lofty response: 'On the golf-course, as in my trade, I am a loser most of the time. Why should I be grudged delight in a rare triumph?'

The Padre was inclined to be euphoric, too, praising his eldest son for being 'a real MacVicar'. He now revealed that members of his family had always been good at telling stories.

My mother was happy. 'I always knew you'd be a famous writer,' she said to me. With a glance across the tea table at the Padre, she added: 'Did you know that my great-uncle on my mother's side once published a book of Gaelic poetry?'

The Padre snapped at the bait like a cruising shark. 'One of the greatest Gaelic poems ever to come out of North Uist was *Oran Chlann a Phiocair*, "Song of the Clan MacVicar", written in the sixteenth century by an ancestress of mine. And when I come to think about it, what about Sir Walter Scott's friend, Mrs Grant of Laggan, who wrote *Letters from the Mountains*, the eighteenth-century classic? She was a MacVicar.'

'But not,' remarked my mother, 'a North Uist MacVicar.' Then, inconsequently, she announced: 'I had another great-uncle who designed bridges for the Czar of Russia.'

I think it pleased them that *The Purple Rock* was dedicated 'To My Father and Mother'. Hebridean insistence upon 'honouring thy father and mother' conforms, of course, with biblical teaching; but I am sure it stems originally from ancient laws which held that reverence for parents was necessary in creating a strong sense of 'family'.

It distresses me to hear someone say about parents, 'I didn't ask to be brought into this world. They indulged themselves to get me born. Why should I show them any more consideration than anyone else?' That is a direct quote from an acquaintance of mine in a London office. Needless to say, he shows little consideration for anybody, let alone his widowed mother. I believe he has overlooked the fact that, apart from the material benefits of food, clothing and education during his helpless years, his parents were also responsible for providing him with the greatest gifts of all, those of life and love. Is a little love and respect in return too much to ask? Is a happy and united family not the very foundation of a happy and united society?

The idea so often bandied about in modern society that the state should be responsible for the upbringing of children, leaving parents to pursue their jobs as labelled state employees, brings me to the edge of horror. Do those who advocate it realize that they are marching down a narrow road straight into the arms of Big Brother?

Rona, my brothers and Maimie were all glad about *The Purple Rock* but not, I think, greatly impressed. Neither was Jean. Neither were my neighbours in Southend. It became clear that their interest in me was as a person, not as an author; and eventually, by recognizing this, I was able to plant my feet more firmly on the ground. In a vague kind of way it was revealed to me that in a small community one earned affection and respect not by being brilliant at a particular job but by one's attitude and behaviour in relation to other people.

In the contract drawn up between Stanley Paul & Co., Ltd. on the one hand and A. M. Heath & Co., Ltd. and myself on the other, it was agreed that the novel should be published in hardback within six months at 7s 6d. Royalties would be paid to me (through Heath) at the rate of ten per cent on the first 2500 copies sold, fifteen per cent on the next

2500 copies sold and twenty per cent on all copies sold above 5000. I was to receive an advance on royalties of £25, payable on the day of publication. If the book was later published in a paperback edition priced at 6d, the royalty would be 15s per thousand copies sold. Ten per cent of all monies due to me would be retained by Heath.

The contract was signed for and on behalf of Stanley Paul & Co., Ltd. by F. A. Cowling, Director. With a flourish I signed for and on behalf of 'the author'.

Twenty-five pounds didn't seem a large advance; but I calculated that once *The Purple Rock* had sold over 5000 copies – as I was certain it would – and the royalty rate had soared to twenty per cent, I would be in sight of my first Rolls-Royce. And what if somebody published it as a serial, or even made a film of it? The possibilities were as wide and uncertain as the waves breaking on the shore.

There was one snag, however, as there always is for writers bemused by pleasurable dreams. My typescript contained only 60 000 words. Frank Cowling indicated in a friendly way – betraying only that slight hint of steel which, in the future, I came to recognize as the publisher's secret weapon – that he would like me to add 'at least' 10 000 words to it, so that it might 'approximate more closely' to the 'usual length required in a novel'.

I faced the task with confidence. For the next fortnight, after my day's work with the *Courier*, I sat down each evening in Mrs Rankin's front room to write 1000 words, mostly great swatches of 'scenic description' composed, as I imagined, in a vein of poetry. I also enlarged upon the thoughts passing through the minds of my characters and succeeded, on the whole – though I didn't, of course, realize it at the time – in clogging up the action of what had been planned as a fast-moving thriller. But when I sent the revised typescript to Frank Cowling he declared himself satisfied and, joyfully, I returned untrammelled to my reporting duties and awaited with impatience the publication of 'my book'.

In the spring of 1933 the proofs came and were corrected at speed. Dust jacket designs were sent to me for approval. I chose one picturing a glamorous girl in a tartan frock perched somewhat incongruously on a seaside rock. She had blonde hair, whereas my heroine was a brunette (like Jean); but Frank Cowling explained to me that a blonde would sell the book better than a brunette and that, in any case, there were technical difficulties in reproducing brunettes in colour. I did not argue with him.

Then I was told that publication had been fixed for the last week of May. I suggested to Alec MacLeod that I might write a piece about it for 'Sparks and Flashes'. Generously he allowed me to do so but began looking at me with his head on one side, possibly in much the same way as a suspicious hedge sparrow regards a fledgling cuckoo in the nest.

Excitement grew. My work on the *Courier* did not suffer. Indeed, the reverse took place. I wrote my pieces with abounding energy and enthusiasm. Slowly recovering from the loss of his wife, Alec took more and more time off to write his 'Neonach' articles. During this period – for once – the paper was discussed favourably in Kintyre.

A month before the magic date in May, six advance copies of the book arrived, free of charge, for the author. This is normal practice, usually covered by a clause in the contract. For me it was anything but normal. When I tore open the parcel and set eyes upon my 'baby', I think I understood what a mother must feel as she looks upon her first-born. It was a beautiful book. I said so, and everybody agreed with me. Few would be able to resist buying it. I said that, too, and again everybody agreed with me. The word 'vainglorious' must have stirred in the minds of all my relatives and friends.

One jarring note was struck by Miss Annie Morgan, who kept a bookshop in Campbeltown. Straight grey hair and a thin, bespectacled face were camouflage for a generous nature. Her conversation was sharp, earning her a reputation as a female Wyatt Earp who always shot from the hip. She saw my heroine on the dust-jacket, did a double-take, then sniffed and said: 'Angus, why on earth is your girlfriend wearing a tartan goonie?' ('Goonie' is an old-fashioned

Scots word, meaning 'nightie'.) I tried to ignore a sudden
conviction that the sophisticated frock which might have
looked appropriate at a Caledonian Ball in London was out
of place against a background of Scottish rocks and sea and
sky. I was glad to discover, however, that Miss Morgan did
not hold my heroine's clothes against me. She ordered two
dozen copies of the book from a delighted traveller – and,
in due time, two dozen more, all of which she was able to
sell.

Later on she and Jean became friends. When they got
together I was frequently lectured on my behaviour in dictatorial terms. Like Kubla Khan, Miss Morgan was inclined
to class me as a lazy writer and hounded me on to increase
both the quantity and the quality of my work. She often
criticized my books to my face; but I was told that if anybody
came into her shop and spoke evil words concerning them,
she would react like a wild cat protecting her young.

While I was away from home during World War II she
often stayed at Achnamara, keeping Jean company and writing letters filled with hard-headed advice that would have
done credit to Samuel Smiles. We still have the Tusitala
edition of Robert Louis Stevenson and the ancient grandfather clock which she bequeathed to us when she died.

Frank Cowling did what I know now to have been an
excellent job of providing publicity for *The Purple Rock*. He
had small postcards printed showing a picture of my heroine
alongside a copy of the boastful 'blurb' composed by the
author. A packet containing twelve dozen was sent to me,
and I had a happy time posting cards to addresses picked
from a telephone book. On a visit to Glasgow I left some
lying on the seats of tram-cars and laid a paper-trail of them
through Kelvingrove Park. I then invaded the cloisters of the
university and scattered about a dozen around the door of
the political economy lecture-room. 'Put that in your pipe
and smoke it, Adam Smith!'

On the Sunday before publication large advertisements
appeared in both the *Sunday Times* and the *Observer*. They
were set in the bold, black type which, at the time, was
characteristic of the Hutchinson group of companies: bold,

black type entirely pleasing to authors panting for recognition.

THE PURPLE ROCK
by
ANGUS MACVICAR

For sheer excitement and dramatic tension there are chapters in this novel which have seldom been surpassed in modern fiction. One of the most readable and entertaining books ever written by a Scottish author.

Stanley Paul & Co., Ltd., price 7/6d net.

By this time I had almost forgotten that such resounding praise had been born of my own dreams. Like Dr Goebbels, I was beginning to believe in propaganda initiated by myself. This may have been one reason why publication day proved anti-climactic.

That morning I went into the *Courier* office with high expectations. What did I expect? Congratulations? A celebration cake? A guard of honour? In the outcome nothing happened. Jenny, Isa and Cathie in the shop said 'Hullo' and went on with their business of selling newspapers and pencils and exercise books and paper doylies. As I passed into the composing room Archie MacMillan, at the keyboard of the linotype, expertly spat out a stream of tobacco-juice which, as usual, landed only a few inches away from my highly polished shoes. 'Hi!' he said, amid clattering machinery and the fumes of hot lead. Big Peter and Arthur Henderson were engaged in 'dissing' type from the previous week's *Courier* and uttered only their customary grunts of welcome. Alec sent me out to interview the Provost, who was introducing a controversial piece of local legislation at that evening's Town Council meeting. Nobody mentioned *The Purple Rock*.

To some extent the day was saved by Miss Morgan. As I passed her shop in mid-morning I saw my book placed in a central position in the window. Stopping to admire it, I was summoned inside by an imperious voice. 'Come and sign some copies, Angus. Help to sell them.' With jumping pulse and no small amount of pride I did as I was told.

During this happy session I was introduced by Miss Morgan to several customers, one of whom, marvellous to relate, actually bought a copy of the book. To witness the sale of his own product is perhaps the author's greatest thrill. That day I was enchanted. Even now, forty-six years and sixty-nine books on, when, like a poor man's Edward Heath, I go around the bookshops and sign copies for queues of beautiful customers, I am still enchanted. In fact, recognizing that it gives an author pleasure to see his work being sold for hard cash, Lavinia Derwent and I attend each other's signing sessions, buy each other's books and demand each other's autograph. *A Breath of Border Air* in exchange for *Salt in My Porridge* – what could be more appropriate?

But then, as I completed my signing stint in Miss Morgan's shop, reality returned. Willie Smith, the expert on bramble jam, came bustling in. He scarcely glanced at the book I tried to show him. 'Come ootside, Angus. I've a rare tare tae tell ye aboot auld Sammy Mitchell. It's no' jeest a "spark", it's a "flash" as weel!' First things first. I got on with my job as a reporter.

A cheque for £22-10s arrived by post the next day. This represented the advance on royalties, less Heath's ten per cent. I withdrew all my savings from the post office and proceeded to open an account with the Bank of Scotland. It seemed to me appropriate that an author should deal with a dignified bank manager, who always acknowledged a customer's individuality, rather than with a brash and sometimes dictatorial post office clerk.

For forty-six years now I have been a customer at the Campbeltown branch of the Bank of Scotland. Managers like Albert Smith, Norval Charteris, Ian Rattray and Hamish McKinnon have all been friendly, in spite of the fact that frequently my current account has been overdrawn. Their help and advice – and practical encouragement in difficult times – has been invaluable to a temperamental author who can scarcely count up to ten, even on his fingers.

Not long ago I acquired a few shares in the Bank of Scotland and am intrigued to be called, after a hoary custom, a 'proprietor'. From impecunious reporter to 'proprietor' of a bank. 'Whaur's yer Andrew Carnegie noo?'

With *The Purple Rock* safely launched, albeit with a minimum of local acclaim, I decided it was time to buy a car.

Next door to the *Courier* Office was a garage owned by John Huie & Co., Ltd. I went round to see my friend, Jack Huie, who beamed at me and said: 'I have the very thing for you. A second-hand 1926 bull-nose Morris. Going at seven pounds ten.'

She looked to me like a bargain, with her touched-up green paint, canvas hood, mica screens and polished blunt nose pointing towards the garage wall. 'May I have a go in her before I decide?'

'Sure. Get in. I'll crank her up for you.' Jack went round and inserted the starting-handle.

I had only once before driven a car, a T-model Ford belonging to Hamish Taylor's father, in which Hamish and Lachie Young and Archie and I sometimes travelled to Highland Games. But I was confident I could handle a Morris equally well.

Jack got the engine started. I manipulated the choke in expert fashion.

'Reverse her a bit,' said Jack, his back to the wall. 'Then you can drive straight out.'

I juggled with the gear-lever, heard a satisfactory click and put my toe on the accelerator. In a moment the garage was filled with wild yells and imprecations. Instead of reverse I had engaged first gear. Lurching forward, the car had pinned Jack against the wall. Fortunately the mudguards had taken the main force of the impact. He was unharmed, in physical if not in spiritual terms.

I found reverse and released my friend. 'Sorry,' I said. 'I'll just have to buy her after that, won't I?'

'Take her away,' he groaned. 'And don't come back here until you learn to drive.'

That evening, the old bull-nose shuddering at her top

speed of 40 m.p.h., I drove down to Southend and took my mother and Jean out for what we called a 'spin': a 'spin' enjoyed in carefree circumstances almost unimaginable to modern motorists. Driving tests and MOT tests were unknown, mere glints in some bureaucrat's eyes. Petrol could be had for less than a shilling a gallon. As we chugged our way along the steep, unfenced road to the Mull of Kintyre, no other car moved within miles of us. Curly horned black-faced ewes scuttered away among the heather, which, at this time of early autumn, was burgeoning into great masses of purple. When we stopped at the Gap, high above the lighthouse, the sun was shining and the Irish hills were smokey blue across the North Channel. The only sounds were those that came from bleating sheep and from the larks which sang, soaring, 'in the clear air'. Life was free and exciting, and I rejoiced to be part of it.

During that summer more rejoicing occurred. Edward Shanks gave *The Purple Rock* a column review in the *Sunday Times* – a review which included my picture – while Compton Mackenzie wrote a long article about it in the *Daily Mail*. In the first chapter of my novel the hero is discovered reading a book by Compton Mackenzie; but I am certain this had nothing to do with the future literary knight's generous treatment of a young author.

Then Stanley Paul began to advertise *The Purple Rock* as being in its 'third impression'. I had no idea then what was meant by an 'impression'. Even now it remains a mystery to me, though I have an idea it can indicate anything from 500 copies to 5000, depending on the original print order. It sounded good, however, and, the wish being father to the thought, I inferred that my book had reached the best-seller class. I made up my mind that, after all, I was going to succeed in my ambition to become a freelance writer and told Alec MacLeod that later in the year I might be leaving the *Courier*. He looked glum. 'Don't make up your mind just yet,' he advised. 'See how things turn out.'

Things did not turn out as well as I imagined. In cold figures, *The Purple Rock* sold no more than 2000 copies in hardback. As I now realize, this was a fairly satisfactory

result for a pre-war first novel; but it earned me less than
£75, which meant that my plan to exchange the bull-nose
Morris for a Rolls-Royce had to be postponed.

Later on, the book was published as a Toucan paperback
at 6d (Toucans were Hutchinson's answer to Allen Lane's
popular Penguins), and this brought in another £21, which
wasn't at all bad, representing as it did, at 15s per thousand
copies, a sale of 30 000. A literary syndicate, the name of
which I can't remember, acquired the serial rights and, in
abbreviated form, the story appeared in, amongst other papers, the *Daily Record* and the *Irish Free Press*. My cut from
the serial sales was £15.

Total income from *The Purple Rock* amounted, therefore,
to £111, which, as it contained about 70 000 words, meant
that if future books sold at the same rate I could count on
earning approximately thirty shillings per thousand words.
Writing a thousand words each day, which already I had
found to be no great hardship, I could look forward to a
weekly income of at least £7, more than double what I was
getting with the *Courier*.

So I calculated, putting aside all consideration of the many
booby-traps that litter the road of a freelance writer – illness,
lack of inspiration, fickle editorial policies, irregular times of
payment and almost total lack of security, to name, as they
say, but a few. But independence beckoned. With the prospect of becoming my own master dangling before me like a
super carrot, there was no way that Alec MacLeod, in spite
of our friendship, was going to keep me as an employee. No
Rolls-Royce, as yet, but plenty of jam on my piece. And who
could tell when a film offer might come?

Frank Cowling once told me that at this period, almost fifty
years ago, works of fiction poured out from the presses 'like
bullets from a Gatling gun', which was a favourite simile
employed by contemporary 'thrill' merchants. It had something to do, he said, with keeping printers in work. The
average sale of a first novel – and, indeed, of second and
third novels – was around 700, a point at which the publisher
only narrowly avoided a loss. Why *The Purple Rock* should

have sold about three times that number is still not clear to me. I suppose, to use political language, there were various contributory factors.

Nowadays, thrillers with a Scottish background are 'thick as autumnal leaves that strow the brooks in Vallombrosa'; but in 1933 they were rarer birds. George Blake himself had written one or two under a pseudonym, while a few serial story writers got their Scottish thrillers published in book form. On the whole, however, Scotland's main exponents of the *genre* were still considered to be Robert Louis Stevenson and John Buchan. A number of reviewers compared my work, not unfavourably, with that of both those writers; and this may have helped to sell my book.

My good fortune in obtaining long and kindly reviews from Compton Mackenzie and Edward Shanks was another factor. The pundits tell me that reviews do not greatly affect the sales of books: what matters is that people should talk about them and recommend them to one another. But what starts people talking? Surely a good review, given plenty of space, can be part of the answer?

The trouble, for a beginning author, is to get his book mentioned at all. Today, about a hundred books are published every working day in Britain: books divided by the trade into forty-four separate categories, from 'aeronautics' through 'fiction' to 'wireless and television'. In *The Publishing Game* Anthony Blond calculates that one new novel is published every twenty minutes. It follows, therefore, that the literary editors of newspapers and magazines (by whom copies received for review are sent out to the reviewers) are constantly surrounded by heaving masses of books all awaiting attention, and a beginning author has to depend upon sheer luck to have his 'baby' catch their eye. In 1933 the spate of new fiction was even more swollen than it is now; and as I grow wiser in the ways of publishing, my luck in having had *The Purple Rock* featured in the *Sunday Times* and the *Daily Mail* becomes ever more astonishing.

I think Frank Cowling's advertising of *The Purple Rock* also contributed to a reasonably successful launch. The advertising of books at the present time is on nothing like the scale habitual in 1933, except perhaps in the case of new stories by such 'block-busters' as Arthur Hailey, Jack Higgins (Harry Patterson), Alistair MacLean and Harold Robbins – and even they have the benefit of the additional publicity generated by the filming of their books. But by 1933 standards, *The Purple Rock* was given unusual space in newspapers ranging from *The Sunday Times* and the *News Chronicle* to the *Glasgow Herald*, the *Scotsman* and the *Aberdeen Press and Journal*. Then there were the postcards, exhibiting my tartan-clad heroine, which I like to think sold a few hundred copies by themselves.

Publishers with whom I have discussed the subject all declare that, like reviews, advertising makes little difference to the sales figures. What I suspect they mean is that the cost of advertising has become so high that it can be viable only if a book promises to be a best-seller. After all, a four-inch double column in, for example, *The Sunday Times* or the *Observer* costs something like £400, which may be more than the publisher is paying his thriller writer as an advance on royalties. But the question remains: how can a book become widely known and, therefore, talked about, if potential readers are not even told that it exists?

Apart from reviews and advertising, in 1933 other methods of making a book known included reference to it in trade journals, gossip columns and, best of all, the news. Agents, publishers and booksellers, when they felt inclined, were often successful in getting their more important books mentioned in the trade journals and gossip columns. They found it more difficult to turn their authors into subjects for investigation by news reporters. Sometimes, however, miracles occurred.

As a teenager, I was intrigued to learn, along with millions of other newspaper readers, that Agatha Christie had gone missing. The titles of the few books she had written at the time were mentioned in every report of her disappearance. Apparently the case was a genuine one, concerned with temporary loss of memory; but I am sure no press agent could have found a better method of establishing Agatha Christie as the most successful thriller writer of the century.

The work of another writer of the period, Mary Webb, was publicly acclaimed by the then prime minister, Stanley Baldwin. From being an obscure author, whose work sold sluggishly, she became, almost overnight, a household name, and her grim tales of country life, notably *Gone to Earth*, galloped on the back of newspaper publicity into the high peaks of best-sellerdom.

I envied both those ladies their success in terms of sales and wondered if some day, by happy chance, I might get my name in the news. I never did, to any profitable extent. My life-style has seldom been newsworthy; and press agents have always been luxuries beyond my purse. But I have never been 'blate', as we say in Scotland, to jump at any chance of free publicity.

One day, playing golf with three friends over Dunaverty, my home course, I had a hole in one. Before the customary celebrations could blur my faculties I telephoned the story – as from the *Courier* – to several newspapers. Next morning it duly appeared, alongside advertisements (already booked) which made known that my new children's novel, *The Grey Pilot*, had just been published and that in the afternoon I should be signing copies at Lyons Bookshop in Sauchiehall Street, Glasgow. The combined operation was a success. The autographing session proceeded merrily, with children and their parents, in a queue of encouraging length, congratulating me on my prowess as a golfer.

As it happens, Lyons in Sauchiehall Street no longer exists. It was destroyed in a curious accident. A laden lorry careered down the steep hill opposite and plunged across the street, like a rogue tank, straight into the bricks and mortar of the shop.

A timely parable? Perhaps. But that is another story.

Today, the basic principles of making new books known are similar to those current in 1933, though the means employed, of course, have undergone change. Newspaper coverage has been overtaken in importance by coverage on radio and television; and there is a wild scramble by authors and publishers to have their wares – and themselves – given prominence on the 'wireless' or on the 'goggle-box'.

But luck plays a part here, too. For example, consider the good fortune of William Collins Sons & Co., Ltd., when, at the same time, they published *Doctor Zhivago* and the *Memoirs* of Field-Marshal Sir Bernard Law Montgomery. Both books became the subject of news stories, Pasternak refusing to accept the Nobel Prize and 'Monty', true to his admirably abrasive character, directing schoolboy raspberries at Eisenhower's qualities as a general. Radio and television made a hearty meal of both controversies; and I am told that, as a result, Collins enjoyed a million-pound turnover in one month.

In my own small world of book-writing, I have always had help from fellow Scottish journalists, as happened in the case of my hole in one. They are the most generous people I know. When they can, they give news of my books space in their papers and have never, in my experience, betrayed the 'I kent his faither' syndrome or the slightest hint of envy or jealousy. Not that they have anything to be envious or jealous about, as far as my material condition is concerned. Most of them, like my son Jock, earn about three times as much as I do. There must be times, however, as they slog away at their typewriters in hot and narrow offices, praising the work of some suddenly successful author – like Alistair MacLean, for example – when envy for someone who has now achieved freedom from authority and from deadlines must raise a cobra head. But I have never known them allow it to escape.

Sometimes they harbour criticisms of my work, which they express to me in private. But, like good family men and women, they are loath to denigrate a brother Scot in public. As one continuously obsessed by envious and jealous neuroses, I salute them. Britain might be a happier place if certain politicians followed their example and ceased to blackguard their countrymen in the hearing of the world at large.

Why any book sells well depends in part upon a complex mixture of good publicity and good luck. But when all is said and done (as the Padre used to say when a thundering sermon approached its climax), perhaps the most important considerations concern (a) the ability of the author to 'share his thoughts and impressions with the crowd' and (b) the ability of the publisher's rep to share his enthusiasm for the book with the booksellers.

Hutchinson's chief rep in Scotland is Bob Cowan, a happy, friendly man whose golf swing is suspect but whose professional swing is sharp, incisive and a thing of beauty to those authors whose books he works so hard and so successfully to sell. With Bob Cowan in charge, who needs a press agent? When *Rocks in My Scotch* was published in 1977, he arranged for it a programme of publicity which left me limp but which he described, snarling a little, as a run-of-the-mill operation. In the programme, which took place over two days, I submitted to five separate meetings with newspapermen and photographers, a phone-through interview with BBC Radio in London, a talk-in with Jameson Clark for Radio Scotland's 'Good Morning, Scotland', an hour-long interview broadcast later by Radio Clyde, an appearance in a film made by STV, four signing sessions in various Glasgow bookshops and several meals with influential booksellers. Jean was brought into the action, too, providing a 'Woman's Page' with candid and, to me, somewhat startling comments about my domestic behaviour.

Being shy and lazy, a lover of the quiet life, I found that the only enjoyable part of the experience was meeting my fellow workers in the various media and talking shop with them. There is no question, however, that it helped not only to sell the book in Scotland but also to reinforce my shaky self-esteem as an author. I went through it willingly, as much for Bob's sake as for my own. He is proud of his salesmanship. He ought to be. So should Hutchinson. He could sell fish to the seals which bob up and down in the sea outside my window.

In the book world confident sales projections are the cause of many an accountant's duodenal ulcer. A book of high quality produced by the most prestigious publisher, recommended to booksellers by the most skilful reps, provided with coverage in newspapers and on radio and television by the most skilful PROs, given rave reviews and expensive advertising – such a book may still fall down and break its crown.

Sphere, the paperback publishers, paid £27 000 for Len Deighton's *Only When I Larf*. They printed 300 000 copies, gave it the works as far as publicity was concerned but, in the end, sold only 100 000. In a quiet backwater of publishing the University of London Press produced a slim volume called *English in Libya*. I imagine the reps did a lot of good work here; but there were no reviews, no publicity, no advertising. It sold 230 000 copies – and still sells.

Names and Addresses, an autobiography by Tom Mathews (once editor of *Time* magazine) was the subject of wide advertising and received excellent reviews, not only in the quality Sunday papers but also – on account of some scandal-skirting stories it retailed concerning the publishing tycoon Henry Luce – in the popular tabloids. It did not sell. *The Godfather*, by Mario Puzo, was meagrely advertised and ignored by reviewers but gradually became a super block-buster all over the world. Putnam's, New York, were the original publishers of *The Godfather*. The editor-in-chief, Bill Targ, was asked if he had anticipated such an enormous success for the book when he first published it. He said: 'I knew it was good, but I didn't believe it could be all *that* good!'

A horror story is told in *The Oxford University Press: An Informal History* which always makes me feel better when I worry about the sales of my books. In 1879, Oxford published a bulky volume, translated from the German, on passerine birds. (*Passer* in Latin means a sparrow. Passerine describes a huge order of perching birds, all sparrow-like in shape.) The trade was enthusiastic and the book warmly recommended by no less an authority than Charles Darwin. It sold seven copies in its first year, one in its second, and thirteen more in the next twenty-three years. Spare a few tears for the German author, but none for Oxford. In 1881 the firm's Revised Version of the New Testament sold a million copies on publication day.

All my writing life I have aimed at producing a best-seller. The pressures of living, the need to earn money to support a family and a comfortable home makes it almost inevitable that an author should think in this way. But it is something, I now believe, that a genuinely dedicated author should never do, and it may explain my comparative lack of credibility as an 'important' one.

In the fifties, when my stories for children about the Lost Planet were being broadcast as BBC radio and television serials and syndicated as strip cartoons before being published in book form by Burke, I almost made the grade. *The Lost Planet* and it sequel *Return to the Lost Planet* both sold around 15 000 copies in hardback – and that, as Bob Cowan might put it, ain't hay! Especially when there is evidence that in those immediate post-war days many booksellers, rendered smug by a long spell of easy selling during the black-out, were by no means as efficient and on the ball as their modern counterparts.

I remember once, in 1952, visiting a Glasgow bookshop (now under new and more lively management) and inquiring politely of a female executive why none of my books appeared to be on sale. 'Get yourself on the wireless,' she told me, pertly. 'Better still, have your books *read* on the wireless. Then we'll sell them all right.' My books weren't being *read* on the wireless, but they *were* being broadcast in the form of at least two six-part serials a year, not only in Scotland but throughout the United Kingdom and abroad. I didn't argue with the lady. What was the use? She neither knew nor cared. But Bob Cowan, I suspect, would have reacted in a more positive way.

The purpose of all this rambling, sometimes inconsequential comment is to prove that *nobody knows why any book sells well or badly*. Cunning old professionals advise that sex, money and religion, with doctors and nurses lurking in the background, are the main ingredients of a potential bestseller. This may be true, but plenty of books containing all these ingredients still moulder on remainder shelves. An author, in my opinion, may be compared to the famous submarine commander who navigated 'by guess and by God'.

Take the case of *Salt in My Porridge*.

The LOST PLANET

.... AND WHEN YOU'VE DONE THAT, SEE PROFESSOR BERGMAN — HE'S WORKING ON THE ROTARY JETS .... ASK HIM TO BRING THE BLUE PRINTS AND DISCUSS THEM WITH ME AT SIX O'CLOCK !

YES, UNCLE .... BUT ... WHAT ARE THOSE ROTARY JETS FOR ?

WHAT !! HAVEN'T YOU GRASPED THAT YET ?

I WILL PUT IT SIMPLY, JEREMY. AS WE JOURNEY INTO SPACE, THE PULL OF GRAVITY BECOMES LESS, AND IF SOMETHING WERE NOT DONE, WE SHOULD DRIFT ABOUT INSIDE THE SHIP ! HELPLESS !

53

IF WE SET THE SHIP SPINNING AROUND THIS CENTRAL SHAFT BY MEANS OF LOW POWER ROTARY JETS IT WILL CREATE ARTIFICIAL GRAVITATION.

54

NO-ER-!

WELL, ASK PROFESSOR BERGMAN! I'VE NO TIME! AND DON'T STAND THERE GAPING. SEE JANET AND THE PROFESSOR .... AND DON'T LOITER ON THE WAY!

HIS UNCLE'S INSTRUCTIONS CARRIED OUT, JEREMY ENQUIRES ABOUT THE ROTARY JETS ....

THEY'RE SO SMALL.... NOT LIKE THE DRIVING JETS!

SO THAT'S WHY THE SHIP IS MORE SQUAT THAN A TORPEDO?

YES! AND THE SPIN WILL BE CONTROLLED, OF COURSE, SO THAT OUR WEIGHT IS THE SAME AS ON EARTH .... WE SHALL WALK ON THE INNER HULL — HEADS TOWARDS THE SHAFT ....

JUST LIKE THE ROTOR AT BATTERSEA PLEASURE GARDENS!

YES! BUT MORE COMFORTABLE AS THE SHIP IS LARGER!

As I approached the OAP stage – and, in consequence, for the first time in my life basic financial security – I decided to write a book which would show that Jean and I were grateful to our families and friends for their kind care over the years. In addition, I wanted to demonstrate that in our case, unpopular though the idea has become in a modern permissive society, family life based on the Christian ideal is still a main source of happiness. I wrote *Salt in My Porridge* in two months, letting it come out of my heart rather than my head. I didn't think it would sell more than a few hundred copies. Nor did I care. I had written it to please myself.

Gerald Austin of Hutchinson was not, I think, too sure about its sales potential, either. The first print order was for 3000 copies.

On the date of its publication in February 1971 a post office strike blanketed all communication by mail. Here in Southend, lacking any kind of documentary evidence as to the book's reception and progress, I suspected that it had been still-born. Even my cheque for the advance on royalties, payable on publication, was lost, temporarily, in the stagnant pool of some sorting office in London.

Then one day I had a phone-call from Gerald. 'Angus, we're reprinting. From all the signs it seems we have a minor best-seller on our hands.'

When the post office strike ended, the happy fact emerged that *Salt in My Porridge* had been received with kindness by several critics and was being bought in surprising numbers not only by the libraries but also by individuals. Eventually it sold about 11 000 copies in hard covers. It is still selling, now as a Fontana paperback.

Why? A clear answer fails to present itself. But now that I pause to attempt an analysis, I have to admit that the book does have to do with sex, money and religion as well as with doctors and nurses. This was not the result of deliberate planning. It simply happened. That's life, as Esther Rantzen might say.

The first book I wrote to please myself, as an amateur rather than as a professional, became in every way my most successful. Here, it would seem, I ought to add a moral. Unfortunately I'm not quite sure what it is.

9. The Pride of the Peacock

When I told Alec MacLeod, about six months after publication of *The Purple Rock*, that I had decided to give up my job on the *Courier* and become a freelance, he shook his head: 'I'm sorry. If you'd stayed on, the *Courier* would have been yours one day.'

I had a spasm of uneasiness. Had I known about this beforehand, would it have influenced my decision? The *Courier*, with its attendant stationary business, was a small gold-mine. My amateur calculations, based upon some study of the accounts, indicated that it produced an annual profit on turnover of nearly forty per cent. Here was security and the promise of positive financial reward for hard work which would almost certainly be absent from the future of a self-employed author.

But the spasm passed. My ambition was to be my own man, with a life habit removed from dependence on orders and instructions, a life in the country with Jean, where, at our own convenience, we could take time off to smell the flowers. 'I'm sorry, too,' I told Alec. 'And I'll always be grateful for everything you taught me, not only about writing.' I meant it then. I mean it now, though Alec has been dead for more than thirty years.

I have never regretted the chance I missed of becoming a newspaper boss. I like being a boss, and I am told that this becomes only too evident when I work as a producer with the Dunaverty Players, Southend's contribution to amateur drama. I am not sure, however, that I'd like to earn money by being a boss. Why? Like Pontius Pilate, I propose to dispense with an answer.

Years later, after World War II, Jean and I were forced to

make a similar decision: whether to go and live in Glasgow or London where lucrative writing opportunities could more easily be found or to remain in Southend, far from the action, where it was certain that many chances of earning a fast buck would be missed. We stayed in Southend; and I have never regretted that decision, either. Especially, for example, on a quiet summer's evening on the golf course, with the scent of the sea and of damp, newly mown grass about us, and the larks laughing as my deadly enemy, Boskers, misses a yard putt for the match on the eighteenth green.

We do not envy the lot of those who direct cameras in a hot studio or pore over dubious headlines in a computerized composing room. They are being well paid for what they are doing. We are not being paid at all for what we are doing. But we earn enough to get by, and hard work can be done when it is raining or after darkness falls. On the face of it, the appropriateness of the following quotation from the works of P. G. Wodehouse may be questioned. But let its significance sink in. 'A good woman is a good woman, but a good drive is a slosh!'

Having said goodbye to the *Courier* – though I did occasional unpaid work for Alec during the next few years – I settled down at the Manse again to pursue my chosen profession. Two books a year was the programme and, not without toil and tears, I was able to sustain it until 1939, when the war came. Sometimes I missed a contract deadline; but Frank Cowling of Stanley Paul was understanding and continued to encourage me.

Frank was good looking – and kind with it – a publisher who took a personal interest in his authors. In his private thoughts he may have agreed with Michael Legat, who, in *Dear Author*, calls them 'fickle, temperamental, unreliable, vain and greedy'. In public he maintained patience and courtesy and never once expressed the opinion, attributed to a jocular Sir Frederick Macmillan, that 'publishing would be fun if it weren't for authors'.

Years later, Jean and I were watching *What's My Line* on BBC television, when suddenly Frank appeared in the hot

seat, silver haired now but still as well groomed and charm-
ing as ever. The panel guessed he was an actor, a business
tycoon, a diplomat – even an income-tax collector – but they
failed to identify him as a publisher. When I used to visit him
in London his daughter, Brenda, was at drama school. She is
now one of the best-known character actresses in television.

I remember Frank telling me once that a publisher 'lives
on great expectations of the most nebulous order'. I told him
he had found the perfect phrase to describe not a publisher
at all but an author. In the past fifty years, however, many of
my nebulous expectations have been realized.

My adult thrillers – twenty-eight of them – have all sold
fairly well in this country and in various translations abroad.
I made six of them into radio plays and more than a dozen
into newspaper serials. My children's books have sold well,
too, almost all of them starting life as radio or television
serials.

I am particularly proud of the Hebrew and Japanese edi-
tions of my science fiction stories, taking childish pleasure
from explaining to my young nephews and nieces that, no
matter how it may seem, they have not been placed in my
bookshelves upside down. A Japanese gentleman called
Toho Eizo has expressed interest in making a film of
Super Nova and the Frozen Man; but so far nothing has
come of it.

Many film companies, including Ranks, have 'shown
interest' in my books and, in one or two cases, have even
asked how much I'd want for the film rights. But the 'interest' has always waned. Amongst authors this is a common
experience. I have learned to live with it and to look forward
to success in this direction in much the same detached way as
I look forward to claiming another hole in one at golf.

Sponsored by the Church of Scotland and, later, by the
BBC, I have however, written a number of film scripts. The
most successful, *The Old Padre*, was produced and directed
by the late Ronald Falconer, head of religious broadcasting
in Scotland. It pictured my father exactly as he was, kind and
selfish, irascible and unselfish, a blesser of babies and chas-
tiser of wrongdoers, a chewer of peppermints for 'the wind'

who found God's love in every human thought and activity.

The Old Padre has been shown around the world. A boy-hood friend of mine, Archie MacKay, who emigrated years ago to Tasmania, came in from a day's work on his farm and was shaving in the bathroom. He heard a voice on the television in the living-room and rushed through, calling out to his wife: 'That's Angus MacVicar's voice! I'd know the South-end accent anywhere!'

As the star of the film, the Padre proved slightly difficult whilst it was being made, his time-table being governed by the success or failure of his bowels after breakfast and by his habit of demanding 'a wee sleep' every afternoon. At the time he was eighty-eight years old, and it must be admitted that when he did decide to face the cameras he performed with such natural and unconscious grace that few re-takes were necessary and even the hardbitten technicians in the film-crew were astonished and delighted. Ronnie and I, therefore, remained patient and indulged the star as much as was possible within the bounds of a tight schedule.

The 'wee sleep' in the afternoons presented no real problems. After a hearty lunch at 1.30 p.m., he went to bed at two o'clock and remained there until four. This was a law as of the Medes and Persians, and we planned our shooting programme accordingly. The trouble centred upon the post-breakfast bowel movement. Sometimes this occurred after two cigarettes and the lapse of only thirty minutes. On a bad day, however, at least five cigarettes might be smoked and an hour and a half might go by before we heard the slip-slop of his slippers as he advanced purposefully upon the toilet.

Then, while we waited with our gear and our frustration on the gravel outside, he would emerge at the front door, flushed but triumphant after his exertions, waving a lordly hand. 'Good morning, boys!' he'd greet us – and it must be remembered that anyone under the age of sixty-five was a 'boy' to the Padre. 'Lovely day for the shooting work. Come on, now, better get busy while the sun shines.'

Ronnie and the cameramen, who had perhaps been waiting to do the 'shooting work' for about two hours would meekly follow him as he led the way, stumping and talking, towards the morning's location.

When the film was eventually shown on television he watched it with interest. Afterwards he said to me: 'I was very good. Fortunately I wasn't constipated at the time. You were quite good, too, though maybe a wee bit stuttery. Of course you've got to have the gift.'

How right he was.

During the past twenty years while continuing to write scripts for the BBC and ITV, I have also become a speaker on radio and on the 'box'. Now that I am seventy I may retire from doing this. Fifteen years ago it was brought to my notice that a senior programme planner had declared that at fifty-five I was far too old to be working for the BBC. (Admittedly, I couldn't, at the time, score my age on Dunaverty Golf Course. I can now.) Fortunately, I have other less unimaginative friends in the Corporation, and if I stir myself I am still allowed to compete with younger speakers and script writers. But there comes a time when the bustle and the travelling and the nervous tension before and during a broadcast lose their attraction and the sea air and a game of golf, a local church meeting or exciting drama rehearsal provide more pleasure and satisfaction.

Both Jean and I consider that my writing life, though difficult at times, has been worth while. It has given us independence and the chance to find contentment – and freedom – in a happy community. Occasionally, however, the price of independence and freedom is high.

One such price is an acceptance of the odd belief among neighbours and friends that an author has unlimited time to spare. Jobs on committees, unpaid lectures to societies and clubs of all kinds, writing previews and reports about local events for the press, negotiations with councils, researching family trees for visitors from abroad, entertaining VIPs who come to open new buildings, sales of work, drama shows, etcetera, signing unemployment cards and various other documents for beneficiaries of the state – all such time-consuming activities seem to become his responsibility in spite of every effort to avoid them.

A rubicund farmer on his way to market – and an hour or two in some congenial bar parlour – will wave a lazy hand. 'Och, I'm far too busy to do that. Give Angus the job. He has plenty of time.' When this kind of thing is said in my hearing nowadays, I never hesitate to reply: 'Plenty of time? Do you realize that every time an author stops work to oblige somebody else it costs him money and that he has no means of dunning the Government into recouping his loss? A farm-worker's wages go on, no matter how often he leans back for a chat or a smoke. A farmer's crops go on growing even while he's asleep, and if the crops fail there are subsidies and grants to make up for it.' A few of my hearers have the grace to look slightly embarrassed. The great majority laugh uproariously and slap me on the back, believing that I am making a joke.

Another price paid by a writer of books is that his money (in the form of royalties) always comes in, at the earliest, three months after he has earned it. Some publishers keep him waiting even longer.

But the heaviest burden imposed upon an author is that he is expected to work for nothing in order to benefit the customers of public libraries. Brian Aldiss, chairman of the Society of Authors, has a notable word to say about this, though he does commit the common provincial solecism of using the word 'English' when he means 'British': 'English writers are not paid for the borrowing of their books from public libraries, although the English public library system is the biggest in the western world. Writers are thus compelled to deliver their life-blood as free entertainment.'

The Society of Authors has been campaigning for a Public Lending Right Bill for almost thirty years; but Parliament, while cringing and genuflecting to miners, steel-workers, farmers, ship and car builders – not to mention printers – has continued to cold-shoulder the authors, who, of course, have only minimal voting power at General Elections.

In 1976 we thought we were winning. A PLR bill passed its First Reading and was approved by the Lords. On 14 October, after two earlier adjournments, the bill began its Second Reading in the Commons and, despite the twisting and turning and the filibustering of certain miserable MPs, was approved by a majority. At this point the authors' three main enemies were identified: Roger Moate and Iain Sproat, both Conservatives, and Michael English, Labour. They warned that in committee they would do their best to kill the bill.

They kept their promises, with spates of oratory whose sole purpose was to waste time. On one occasion Iain Sproat (who is, strange to relate, a Scot) jumped to his feet, demanding to know the number required for a quorum. Then he 'suddenly rushed from the room before ascertaining that his absence would not, in fact, hold up the committee, or prevent it from finishing its business for that session'. His tactics were to try and wreck the bill at any price.

Surprisingly, however, the bill completed it committee stage by lunch-time on 9 November, and Report and Third Reading were booked for 16 November, when all available time was to be devoted to PLR.

'Discussion,' according to *The Author*, 'started shortly before 4 pm, when filibustering began again. The three wreckers were joined by five more, so that eight MPs spoke by rota, one overlapping another repeating the same point *ad nauseum*, even if irrelevant to the amendment under discussion. Their main theme was that the bill was badly drafted, and that the 'payment for use' was invalid. Even Phillip Whitehead, a consistent supporter of PLR, spoke for many when he regretted the re-substitution of 'books' for 'works', but argued nonetheless in favour of half a bill rather than none. It was all to no purpose for, in the early hours of Wednesday, 17 November, with mountains of amendments still to discuss and barely two dozen members present, the House voted to suspend the sitting; and so the bill effectively died.'

Another attempt to introduce a PLR bill was made in 1978, but again this came to nothing. In the meantime pious noises in favour of wage rises were being made on behalf of millions of militant trade unionists (and I have no quarrel with that: good luck to all workers wise enough to organize themselves), but scarcely a whisper on behalf of a handful of humble – far too humble – authors.

Perhaps PLR *will* become law one day, though it seems that I, for one, may have been born too soon to benefit by it. In this book, whether bought or borrowed, I would appeal to all fair-minded readers to give thought to the situation. Do you support PLR, or don't you care? If you support it, please tell your MP or local authority, pointing out that if PLR becomes law, writers will be paid not from libraries but from central funds and will receive a small fee each time their work is borrowed. By doing this you will be helping to sustain literature in this country.

As may be deduced from the above, since 1936, when Jean and I built Achnamara and got married, we have spent almost as much time on amateur pursuits as on professional ones.

On the subject of getting married, I think many young people may be startled to learn that our bungalow, built on a quarter-acre site, cost only £700, the garage and a surrounding wall a further £300. Achnamara is now insured for £25 000. Our furnishings were done by the Campbeltown firm of Daniel Mathews, Cabinet Maker, Upholsterer and Removal Contractor. The other day, in a drawer of her desk, Jean came across Mathews's bill, dated 19 December, 1936. Here are some of the items from it:

1 Axminster carpet, 4 yds × 3 yds for lounge	£7-0s-0d
6 yds 72″ brown underfelt	£1-1s-0d
1 Axminster carpet, 3 yds × 3 yds for bedroom	£5-5s-0d
6 yds 54″ brown underfelt	16s-0d
7⅓ sq. yds inlaid linoleum for bathroom	£1-9s-4d
28½ sq. yds inlaid linoleum for hall and kitchenette	£4-9s-9d
Time laying carpets, lino, curtain rods, blinds, etc. (24 hours @ 1/9d, £2-2s; 7½ hours @ 2s, 15s)	£2-17s-0d
Cutting and making 7 pairs net curtains for living room and lounge	6s-6d
Cutting and making 1 pair curtains and vallance for bedroom	2s-6d

1 piano stool	£1-15s-0d
1 kitchen table	£1-15s-0d
1 umbrella stand	11s-0d
1 rose coloured wastepaper basket	5s-0d

Over the years this last item has always been well filled, mainly with copy paper ripped from my typewriter and crumpled into despairing balls. Its clear colour has been tarnished by the smoke of thousands of cigarettes. But at five shillings it has paid its way. So has Jean's piano stool, the umbrella stand and the kitchen table. Perhaps our son Jock, when he becomes an old man, will be able to sell them as antiques.

A young couple setting up home today may be inclined to envy our situation in 1936. It should be remembered, however, that my annual income at the time was only about £350. Inflation and a decimal currency tend to blur the perspective.

Just as a modern permissive society tends to blur one's perspective in regard to religion.

My father was a minister of the Church of Scotland. Jean's father came of a long line of faithful churchgoers. At the beginning there is no doubt we were both bulldozed into attending Sunday School and, later, the church.

On the principle that the son of a strict teetotaller often reacts by becoming a heavy drinker, as a minister's son I could easily have taken a 'scunner' at the Church, which sometimes echoes with negative disciplines. And I confess that when the bulldozing stopped I was often tempted to favour the easy and attractive 'worship in the green fields' policy.

Then I began to understand how much the Church had done – and is still doing – for people in all stations of life. It was a pioneer of education and the social services long before the bureaucrats took over. It still provides the love and sharing care that is sometimes lacking in Government departments. I found that I wanted to be part of it. I found I *wanted* to go to church. And, finally, I found I *liked* going to church. So did Jean. So did Jock, as he grew up.

A communist might argue that we had been 'hooked', victims of 'the opium of the people'. He would be arguing from ignorance, of course, because a communist knows nothing about the freedom of the will, and a professing Christian's condition is that he is faced constantly with having to make choices.

In simple terms, I like going to church because it makes me happy to sing and pray and to share such happiness with other people when all social defences are down and when, for an hour or so, we can all forget the world and be at peace.

When Jean persuaded Barbara, once our daily help, to attend a Christmas service, Barbara enjoyed it, with two reservations. 'Yon solo aboot Jerusalem – I'd far raither it had been *Scots Wha Ha'e*! And I could ha'e been daein' wi' a wee cup o' tea at half-time.'

I agree with Barbara. Black clothes and mournful attitudes seem to me to be out of place at a religious service. Jesus died to make us happy. If we go on moaning and groaning about it, where is the point of His sacrifice?

For me there is happiness and tranquility in a well-filled church and always a new awareness of the dignity of humanity. I am grateful that a Man died to make this possible. And I am sure He would be the last to object if Barbara and Jean and I shared 'a wee cup o' tea at half-time'.

Jean and I joined the church in order to share happiness with others. Because of this I became an elder and Jean a member of the Woman's Guild. We do not claim to be good Christians, but we get occasional glimpses of the light of love. Such glimpses, I believe, are worth working for. And the spiritual faith necessary to sustain Christianity has always been a buttress for the material faith of one author at least in his ability to live by writing.

I am grateful to my parents for many things. Most of all that by precept and example they showed me that religious roads are not haphazard but have been built in the past by men of good will reaching forward towards a satisfying life.

To me, as to many far more gifted writers they are mist shrouded ways, though sign-posts may sometimes be seen, darkly, in the course of determined reconnaissance.

Modern fashionable thought tends to dismiss religion – and the Christian religion in particular – as being a fad for the few, irrelevant to a sophisticated existence. This, I believe, is ignorant thought, uttered without a proper knowledge of the human condition. 'Man,' said Edmund Burke, reflecting on the French Revolution, 'is by his constitution a religious animal.' I think he meant that the human mind is naturally tuned to a religious wavelength, that in spite of frequent oscillations in the wavelength a man cannot escape from it, be he prophet or priest, poet, publican, politician or prole. The desk at which he reads or writes, the hod he carries on a building site, his safety equipment in a coalmine, the tractor he drives when ploughing an open field – everything he sees or touches has a religious significance.

Poets throughout the ages have all acknowledged this. St Columba wrote a *Rune of Hospitality*:

> I saw a stranger yestreen:
> I put food in the eating-place,
> Drink in the drinking-place,
> Music in the listening-place:
> And, in the sacred name of the Triune,
> He blessed myself and my house,
> My cattle and my dear ones.
> For the lark said in her song,
> Often, often, often comes the Christ
>   in the stranger's guise.

William Blake also had a vision of how the mind of carnal man is tuned:

> The pride of the peacock is the glory of God.
> The lust of the goat is the beauty of God.
> The wrath of the Lion is the wisdom of God.
> The nakedness of woman is the work of God.

Robert Burns had a vision, too, though a more homely one:

> Th' expectant wee-things, toddlin', stacher through
> To meet their Dad, wi' flichterin' noise an' glee.
> His wee bit ingle, blinkin' bonnilie,
> His clean hearth-stane, his thriftie wifie's smile,

The lisping infant prattling on his knee,
Does a' his weary care an' kiaugh beguile,
An' makes him quite forget his labour an' his toil.

The trouble with contemporary 'fashionable' thinkers is that they perceive sentiment in religion; and in the late twentieth century sentiment has become something which must be avoided at all costs, being unproductive, materially speaking. And it tends to undermine the authority of the state. But again they are arguing from ignorance and a confusion of thought. Cardinal Newman said: 'Religion, as a mere sentiment, is to me a dream and a mockery.' Mathew Arnold gives a more positive explanation: 'The true meaning of religion is not simply morality, but morality touched with emotion.'

In *The Phenomenon of Man*, Teilhard de Chardin has his own way of supporting St Columba, Blake and Burns in their belief that religion and all ordinary things are woven together: 'Christian love is incomprehensible to those who have not experienced it. That the infinite and the intangible can be lovable, or that the human heart can beat with genuine charity for a neighbour, seems impossible to many people I know – in fact almost monstrous. But whether it be founded on an illusion or not, how can we doubt that such a sentiment exists, and even in greater intensity? ... Is it not a fact, as I can warrant, that if the love of God were extinguished in the souls of the faithful, the enormous edifice of rites, heirarchy and doctrine that comprise the church would instantly revert to the dust from which it rose?'

I believe there is no escape from religion, even in the performance of our prosaic and apparently material daily work. But St Paul has indicated through his letter to the Philippians, how we may cope with the situation. 'Finally, brethren,' he wrote, 'whatsoever things are true, whatsoever things are honest, whatsoever things are just, whatsoever things are pure, whatsoever things are lovely, whatsoever things are of good report; if there be any virtue, and if there be any praise, think on these things.'

From all this philosophical clamjamphrie it has probably

become clear that my religious aspirations are as far from satisfactory fulfilment as the literary aspirations first fertilized by my reading of *The Rudiments of Criticism*. But in both directions I struggle on. I recognize that my best is not good enough, but still I try, panting and peching a little, to achieve it.

10. Murder in Lettermore

I expect I shall die, in the middle of a chapter.

Now that I have reached my 'three score years and ten' I write less desperately than I used to do, avoiding deadlines and ulcer-creating contracts as much as possible. I give myself more time for Jean, for the church, for golf and the drama. But I don't think I will ever retire from writing. For one thing, I'd be miserable if I denied the MacVicar birthright and ceased all attempts to preach and teach and tell stories. For another, I cannot afford to stop, with the old age pension at its present level.

So each morning, after breakfast, I have a walk along the shore, in order to plan the day ahead and to breathe in lungfuls of salty air as an insurance against the cigarette smoke which will surely follow it. Sometimes I find logs and sticks washed in by the tide. I carry them home for sawing into convenient lengths for the fire. Then I sit down and write until lunchtime: 600 words if I am lucky and nobody comes in for a 'crack'.

In the afternoon, if the weather is reasonable, I play golf. (If blizzards blow I remain inside and type out what I wrote in longhand in the morning.) I tell people that I play golf in order to keep fit. The truth is that though I have never been an expert performer I love the game. When I score in less than my age (which, I admit, is not often) it makes me feel that I still retain the vitality necessary to be a writer. When I have a bad round I share my sorrow with Jean, who comforts me into forgetting about it.

In the winter evenings there is the drama. There are church meetings, too, and for Jean the Woman's Guild and the 'Rural'. In the summer evenings there is the garden, with the problems created by onion bugs and carrot fly and the dreadful chore of trying to keep an old lawn tidy. Thankfully, my Atco motor-mower, purchased in 1954, still performs with reliability.

Such continuing amateur endeavour tends to leave me with little time for introspection. But since this book is about me as a writer, I suppose I ought to make an effort at self-analysis. I'll do it my way.

While writing for various media – book publishing, newspapers, radio, television, films, the stage – I have always wanted to tell a story. And it seems, from the evidence, that I am a better storyteller than I am a philosopher.

Before I can succeed in telling an exciting story I must be excited myself, which, I suppose, though I pretend to be a cool professional, betrays an essential amateurism. My first adult thriller, *The Purple Rock*, was born of excitement, the excitement of bringing to life on paper some characters and some places well known to me. So was *The Crocodile Men*, my first Children's Hour radio serial for Kathleen Garscadden, which had as a background Madagascar in time of war. So was *Minister's Monday*, my first film, written for the Church of Scotland about the work of a clergyman. So was *The Lost Planet*, my first television serial, directed in London by Kevin Sheldon. So was *Murder in Lettermore*, my first stage play, commissioned by Bob Christie Park (Argyll County Council's answer to Tyrone Guthrie) for a festival in Duror, the parish of my birth in North Argyll.

Murder in Lettermore is a real-life whodunnit, the most famous (or infamous) thriller in West Highland history. Robert Louis Stevenson heard its echoes and from the bare bones of fact produced *Kidnapped* and *Catriona*.

The story concerns the murder in 1752 of Colin Campbell of Glenure and the subsequent trial of James Stewart of the Glen (*Seumas a Ghlinne*). I heard it first from my mother, a native of Appin, only a few miles from Duror where the murder took place. According to her, James Stewart was falsely accused; but though she claimed to know the name of the real murderer, not even for my benefit would she put a name to him. In the end, after studying a number of relevant

documents, both official and unofficial, I decided to write a
play which would indicate my idea of the truth.

In 1752 James Stewart occupied the farm of Acharn in
Duror. His half-brother, Ardshiel, had been exiled after the
'45; and in consequence James was the recognized leader of
his clansmen. He was in middle life, a practical man of affairs
and a member of the Episcopal Church.

In addition to his own young family, he had reared a boy
called Allan Stewart, the orphan child of a relative. Allan's
by-name was 'Breck', from the Gaelic, meaning 'pock-
marked'. He had taken part in the Jacobite campaign right
up to Culloden and then, like his chieftain Ardshiel, had
escaped to France. From there, with some courage, he
returned at intervals to Duror, to collect for Ardshiel the
secret gifts of his clansmen.

At thirty, Allan Breck was a wild, hard-drinking character; but he seldom missed an opportunity of denouncing the
Campbells, to whose gentle mercies the Hanoverian Government in London had entrusted the West Highlands. One
man in particular was an object of his tirades – Captain Colin
Campbell of Glenure.

Auburn-haired Glenure was nicknamed 'the Red Fox'. He
was, by all accounts, a decent enough man; but to Allan
Breck – and indeed, to all the Stewarts in North Argyll – he
was tainted by three deadly sins. He was a Campbell. He had
fought for the Hanoverians against the Jacobites. And now,
in addition to being laird of Glenure, he had undertaken the
duties of factor on Ardshiel's forfeited estates.

At first, however, James Stewart found him friendly and
easy to get on with. The factor was ignorant in agricultural
matters and had often made use of James's better knowledge. But in the spring of 1752 Glenure was reprimanded by
the Commissioners for the Forfeited Estates for being too
sib with the Stewarts; and, in an unwilling attempt to restore
his authority, he quarrelled openly with James. Allan Breck
was in the neighbourhood at the time, and it is likely that he
encouraged his foster father's resentment.

But worse was to come. A few weeks later, a number of
Ardshiel's Jacobite tenants were ordered by Glenure, on

behalf of the Commissioners, to quit their holdings by Whit Sunday. James immediately championed the cause of his clansmen, broke definitely with Glenure and went to Edinburgh in an effort to procure a suspension of the removing process. On 5 May, however, the Court refused the suspension and James returned to Duror, reflective and dour.

On 14 May, accompanied by his servant, John MacKenzie, and by Mungo Campbell, a lawyer from Edinburgh, and Donald Kennedy, a sheriff officer from Inveraray, Glenure set out from Fort William to carry out the evictions.

On the old road which still winds along the hillside between Ballachulish and Kentallen, the party went in Indian file. As they reached Lettermore ('the hanging coppice') the lawyer was in front on horseback, followed by the sheriff officer on foot and by Glenure and his servant, both riding. It was a beautiful summer day, with warm quiet in the glen. But suddenly, in the green stillness, shots rang out. Glenure fell from his horse with two bullets in his back; and a man with a short, dun-coloured coat was seen escaping along the hillside, carrying a gun. (It was an elaborately wrought long Spanish gun, still called by the Gaelic tale-tellers *An-t-Slinneanach*, 'the gun of the misfortune'.)

Colin Campbell died almost at once, his blood oozing out among the green shoots of bracken. Mungo Campbell remained by the body, but MacKenzie galloped off for help, reaching in a short time the farm of Acharn. There he found James Stewart working in a field and blurted out the news of the tragedy. James stood upright. 'Ah, John,' he said in the Gaelic, 'whoever is the culprit I shall be the victim.'

And so it proved. A well-known Campbell had been murdered in Stewart country. Smouldering hate engendered in the '15 and '45 had once more been fanned into flame. An example must be made. It must be shown that the King's writ could run in Argyll and that Crown factors would be protected or at any rate avenged. Suspicion naturally fell upon Allan Breck, but equally that character had fled to the hills and was on his way to safety in France.

Who next as scapegoat? James Stewart was the man – and James Stewart was arrested.

On 21 September 1752, after spending four months in a filthy jail, he was brought to trial in the old court house at Inveraray. Clad in rumpled broadcloth, he stood in the prisoner's box and watched the jury and the three red-robed judges filing in. Justice was about to be done. Justice with eleven Campbells in a jury of fifteen. Justice with a presiding judge who was none other than Archibald, third Duke of Argyll, head of Clan Campbell and arch-enemy of the Stewarts. Justice which had already allowed possible defence witnesses to be threatened and suborned and even to be held incommunicado during the trial.

'James Stewart, you are indicted at the instance of His Majesty's Advocate and also at the instance of Janet Mac-Kay, relict of the deceased, as being guilty in art and part with Allan Breck Stewart of the murder of Colin Campbell of Glenure.'

When the clerk had finished, Argyll turned to the prisoner. 'What have you to say?'

James Stewart looked at his enemy. 'My Lord, I am not guilty and refer to my lawyers to make my defence.'

Walter Stewart, younger of South-hall, though only a junior counsel, opened for the accused; and his words shine with courage and eloquence even in the dusty records. 'I cannot help complaining of the most intolerable hardships which the panel has undergone since May last. For six weeks no mortal was allowed to see him. After that, indeed, admittance was given to his wife; but his lawyers were carefully denied him until only three days before this trial. His house at Acharn has been searched three separate times and papers carried off by military force, without a warrant. These are hardships which, thanks be to God, meet with no encouragement in this free country.... The panel, enjoying the privileges of every free-born Briton, expects from his judges the greatest impartiality, and the same from the gentlemen of the jury.'

In conclusion he made two submissions. First, that the prisoner, charged only as an accessary, should not be tried until the principal, Allan Breck, was apprehended and found guilty. Second, that the facts and circumstances mentioned in the libel were not sufficient to infer his being an accessory to the murder.

The answer was given by Simon Fraser, a junior counsel for the prosecution, whose legal casuistry would have done credit to his father, the notorious Lord Lovat of the '45. Rebutting the 'plea in bar of trial', he declared: 'It signifies as little what is the law of neighbouring nations, as what was once our own law, if custom, the greatest of all legislators, has now enacted the contrary.'

He went on to give a detailed account of the murder and the causes which led up to it, making his assertions as confidently as if he had been a witness rather than a pleader.

James Stewart and Allan Breck, he said, had uttered public threats against Glenure; but in the end they had decided that the only way to stop his evicting the tenants of Ardshiel was to murder him. 'This plan having been settled, James furnished his friend with a suit of his own – a dark short-coat with white buttons – and, thus equipped, Allan went first to Fasnacloich and then to Ballachulish to await the time when Glenure would cross the ferry on his way into Duror. He questioned the ferryman about Glenure, then immediately ran up the hill, from whence he had a short passage into Lettermore. And it was some time later, my Lords, in this same glen of Lettermore, that Allan Breck Stewart seized his long wished for opportunity, and when Glenure was come within convenient distance this abandoned assassin shot him dead with two bullets from behind –'

At this point, we are told, Simon Fraser stopped abruptly as a youth, dark and wild-eyed, rose shouting from his seat in the public benches: 'It is a lie! I cannot thole it . . .'

Urgent friends silenced the interrupter, who, according to the tale-tellers, was young James Stewart of Fasnacloich. Argyll stared down his long nose. 'Mr Fraser,' he said, 'pray continue.'

Simon Fraser bowed. 'My Lords, I have described the murder. And while Allan Breck pointed the black gun of the misfortune, what of the prisoner here? James Stewart remained at Acharn – and never once offered to go near the corpse. His own preservation was so closely linked with

Allan Breck's that he immediately despatched Alexander Stewart, a kinsman of his own, with money and French clothes to assist the murderer's escape. . . . These, my Lords, are the facts and the circumstances which, I submit, are more than sufficient to infer the crime libelled.'

The court, which consisted of Lord Elchies and Lord Kilkerran in addition to Argyll, then repelled Walter Stewart's two submissions and ordered the trial to proceed.

One of the first witnesses for the prosecution was Alexander Campbell, a dour, heavily built innkeeper from Teynaluib. At the end of April, he said, the prisoner had called at his house on the way to Edinburgh and had been supplied with corn for his horse and a dram for himself. A friend of the witness's had said to James Stewart: 'Give the man of the house a dram in return.' But James Stewart had retorted: 'No, indeed. The only thing I would give a Campbell would be the gibbet!' Witness asked him if he were thinking about Glenure, and James Stewart replied that perhaps he was, and that Glenure had no right to evict tenants from the Ardshiel estates.

Leading defence counsel was George Brown of Coalston, small, pugnacious and widely respected as an advocate. He rose to cross-examine.

'Mr Campbell, you are a man of the world and used to the ways of Highlanders. Didn't it occur to you that James Stewart was joking when he mentioned the gibbet?'

'No, sir. I thought he was in earnest.'

'Come now, did you not part friends?'

'Well, ay, I suppose we did.'

'And James Stewart gave you a dram after all?'

'Ay, but only half a gill.'

Next to give evidence was Mungo Campbell, the young Edinburgh lawyer who had accompanied Glenure on his last journey through Lettermore. 'As we entered the glen,' he said, 'there was a shot. I heard Glenure cry out, "Oh, I am shot!" I dismounted and ran back –' He broke off, sweating and trembling.

The Lord Advocate, William Grant of Prestongrange, raised a sympathetic hand. 'Take it gently, Mr Campbell.'

The witness wiped his forehead. 'Glenure still sat his horse. He said to me, "Take care, he's going to shoot you!" Then I looked up towards the hillside. I saw a man, a man with a short, dark-coloured coat and a gun in his hand. He was running away from me, and though I pursued him at once, he made good his escape. When I returned, Colin Campbell was on the ground. I could see that he was dying, and I sent John MacKenzie into Duror for help. Then he died, and as darkness was coming down I sent the sheriff officer back to Ballachulish. In about an hour he returned with assistance.'

Cross-examining, George Brown underlined the fact that the witness was a nephew of the murdered man's.

He continued: 'Mr Campbell, you say you made out the clothes worn by the murderer as he escaped. Were you close enough to see his face?'

'No, sir.'

'Was he knock-kneed, with a shambling gait?'

'I didn't notice.'

Another prosecution witness was Archibald MacInnes, a big, canny ferryman from Ballachulish. He told how Allan Breck had approached him on the day of the murder, to ask when Glenure would be crossing the ferry. Allan, he said, had been wearing a 'dark-coloured coat, with white buttons', which he identified as belonging to the prisoner.

For the defence, George Brown put only two questions. 'You seem to know Allan Breck fairly well?'

'Och, I've seen him here and there.'

'In that case you can confirm that he is noticeably knock-kneed?'

'Ay, so he is. A feckless-looking cratur.'

Young Donald Stewart of Ballachulish said he had seen Allan Breck on the hillside near Ballachulish House only a few hours after the murder. Allan was wearing a dark coat. He had heard of the murder and was planning to leave the country, because he was afraid he might be accused of it. Being short of money, however, he wanted witness to tell James Stewart at Acharn to send him money and clothes to a place in Glencoe.

'And did you tell James Stewart?' asked the Lord Advocate.

'I told him.'

'And he sent the money to Allan Breck?'

'Ay. On the Sunday it was. I met Alexander Stewart in Glencoe – Alexander Stewart the packman – and he told me he was taking five guineas and some French clothes to Allan Breck.'

In the cross-examination of this witness by George Brown there may be detected odd undercurrents.

'First of all, Mr Stewart – going back to the day before the murder. Did anyone else besides Allan Breck stay at your house that night?'

'Ay. Young Stewart of Fasnacloich.'

'He was a close friend of Allan Breck's?'

Donald Stewart did not answer.

George Brown continued: 'There was a set of young men in Appin – young Fasnacloich, yourself and one or two others – who went about with Allan Breck, publicly condemning the Campbells?'

Again there was no answer, and from the records it would appear that George Brown changed abruptly to a new line of questioning. Had he received a warning glance from the prisoner?

An unwilling witness was James Stewart's servant, Katharine MacColl, who was only sixteen. Nervously she told how on the day after the murder, at Acharn, she had seen the prisoner's wife put a blue side-coat and red waistcoat into a sack.

'You took that sack out on to the moor and hid it?' prompted the Lord Advocate.

'Yes. The packman was to pick it up. But please, sir, my master had nothing to do with the murder. I swear it!'

'That question will be answered by cleverer people than you, my dear. Now, during this summer, when the murder of Mr Campbell was being investigated, did Mrs Stewart tell you not to mention what you knew about the clothes?'

Katharine sobbed. 'She said not to speak about them to strangers.'

Though many other witnesses were put into the box, that, in essence, was the case for the prosecution. A plea by the defence that in justice the case ought to be abandoned for lack of evidence was rejected out of hand by Argyll. Lord Elchies and Lord Kilkerran, cowed by their colleague's stronger personality, spinelessly concurred. In the stuffy court house the trial moved to its inevitable climax.

For the defence, witnesses were few; and it may be significant that though the name of James Stewart, younger of Fasnacloich, appears on the official list, there is no record that he was called.

John Stewart, younger of Ballachulish, said he had never heard the prisoner utter threats against Glenure. James of the Glen was angry when the Ardshiel tenants were to be evicted, but he did not blame Glenure, personally.

'You frequently saw Glenure in the panel's company?'

'Yes. They were always friendly. Only last Hogmanay they drank together at the inn, and on New Year's Day Glenure had dinner at Acharn.'

'James Stewart has a dry sense of humour?'

'Ay. He used to tease Glenure about being a Campbell, and with a long face he would say that all Campbells should be hanged on a gibbet. But Glenure was fit-sides for him. He would turn round and say that the Stewarts should be hanged even higher. Then they would laugh together.'

He added that the prisoner had often helped Allan Breck out of the country before. After the murder, James had said he would do so again, though he did not think Allan had anything to do with the crime.

Simon Fraser rose to cross-examine. 'You are, of course, a Stewart?'

'Ay, and proud of it!'

'You would never betray a member of your clan?'

'Never!'

'Quite so,' said Lord Lovat's son and sat down.

Another witness, Duncan Stewart of Glenbuckie, made the point that he had seen Allan Breck wearing the dun-coloured coat long before the murder. In April, in fact.

George Brown said: 'The prosecution allege that a day or

two before the murder James Stewart gave that coat to Allan Breck, so that he might not be too conspicuous. You are quite sure that you saw him wearing it as early as April?'

'As sure as I am standing here!'

At last it was time for the Lord Advocate to address the jury. He reiterated the case for the prosecution, stressing four major points. First, that James Stewart and Allan Breck, 'conjunct and confident persons', had uttered threats against Glenure. Second, that the murderer had worn a short, dun-coloured coat and that Allan Breck, at the time of the murder, had been wearing a similar garment. Third, that the prisoner had been apprehensive for his own safety. And fourth, that James Stewart and his wife had facilitated Allan Breck's escape by sending him money and French clothes.

But at the end, with a scrupulous fairness which must have irritated the presiding judge, he reminded the jury: 'In all circumstantial evidence there is a possibility of innocence. If you can believe that Allan Breck committed the murder purely on his own accord, then it will be your duty to acquit the panel.'

George Brown spoke for the defence. Squat and grim, aware of the hostile atmosphere in the court, he defied the brooding menace of Argyll.

'Gentlemen of the jury,' he said, 'all along the prisoner has been labouring under a disadvantage. An impression has been industriously raised that the panel, being a Stewart, *must* be guilty, and that if he is acquitted it may be a reflection on this part of the kingdom.'

He went on to state the obvious, that in general all the evidence led by the prosecution broke down at once under examination. 'Nor have they proved that Allan Breck is guilty,' he went on. 'On the contrary, Mungo Campbell admits there was nothing remarkable about the gait of the murderer as he escaped along the hillside; and Allan Breck is notoriously knock-kneed.'

At this point the foreman of the jury, Duncan Campbell of South-hall, interrupted rudely: 'Pray, sir, cut it short! The trial has lasted long enough.'

'Yes, sir,' George Brown blazed back at him, 'it has lasted

long. And if this is your attitude to a man's struggle for his life, then the memory of a great injustice will last even longer!'

In conclusion, defence counsel emphasised the point that Allan Breck was the prisoner's foster son. 'If James Stewart sent him money and clothes after the murder, it was something he had done many times before, the act of a generous and perhaps over-indulgent guardian.'

There was no summing up by Argyll, otherwise known as the Lord Justice General. He knew his men. In a short time the jury brought in a unanimous verdict of guilty. Sentence of death was intoned by the dempster.

In a speech which gives a remarkable insight into his character, Argyll addressed the prisoner: 'James Stewart, we have had a long and most impartial trial, but your guilt is plain. You ate Colin Campbell's bread, then shed his blood. You are one of those incurable enemies of our good and gracious King, stirring up disaffection with every word you speak. Had you and your Highland friends been successful in the rebellion of 1745, you would now have been trampling on the liberties of your fellow subjects. We, who this day are your judges, would have been tried before one of your mock Courts of Judicature and in all likelihood sentenced cruelly to death.'

How often similar speeches have been heard since, in Germany, Russia, Africa, the Middle East, in America, South America and the Far East. And, more's the pity, in the United Kingdom. Political scheming and private hatred are like the bishop-weed in my garden, almost impossible to eradicate.

On 8 November, before a gathering of his countrymen, James Stewart stood beneath a gibbet on *Cnap Chaolis Mhic Pharuig*, near the south end of the new Ballachulish bridge. He met his death with courage, repeating aloud the 35th Psalm, known to this day in the West Highlands as 'James of the Glen's Psalm'.

'I am not afraid to die,' he told his friends. 'But what grieves me is my character, that after ages should think me capable of such a barbarous crime. I declare my complete innocence. Nevertheless, I bear no grudge against the jury and the witnesses; and may this my hard fate put an end to all discords among you. May Stewart and Campbell be united in brotherly love and charity; and may God grant us all a joyful meeting at the Great Day of Judgment.'

Over a hundred years later, John Francis Campbell of Islay collected and wrote down several Gaelic tales relevant to the murder. These were later incorporated in a compendium of Argyll folklore known as the Dewar Manuscripts. According to the Dewar MSS (which, it must be made clear, was a Campbell enterprise), while Donald Stewart of Ballachulish and young James Stewart of Fasnacloich were watching James of the Glen being hanged in chains, Donald had to be restrained by friends from shouting a public confession.

Another of John Francis Campbell's tales provides an interesting sequel. Many years after the murder, when the Stewarts and the Campbells had become friendly again – on the surface, at any rate – Stewart of Ballachulish and Alexander, the brother of Glenure, went shooting together. With his long gun Donald Stewart brought down a stag at long range. Alexander Campbell examined the peculiar double wound in the stag and immediately identified it with the bullet holes in his late brother's back.

'The talk,' says the manuscript, 'produced a coldness between the two. They separated, and each of them chose a road for himself to go home, and they did not henceforth go to hunt together.'

Who shot 'the red fox'?

Allan Breck was charged in his absence with having fired 'the gun of the misfortune', with James of the Glen as an accessary before and after. Allan was certainly capable of such a deed; but, remembering his long experience as a hunted guerilla, I believe that had he done it he would have made a more efficient job of both the killing and the getaway.

My mother's story hinted at a conspiracy hatched by a number of young men in North Argyll, all Stewarts or sib to the Stewarts. This may come near the truth. I reckon that a secret IRA-like meeting was held at which it was decided that Colin Campbell of Glenure, representative of a suppressive and hated regime, should be murdered. Whose gun was best suited to accomplish the killing at long range? And which of the young men should fire it? The long Spanish gun belonging to Donald Stewart of Ballachulish, much superior in every way to weapons of local manufacture, was an obvious answer to the first question. The answer to the second, as I imagine it, was decided by lot. And I think, in common with many another canny storyteller in the West Highlands, that the short straw was drawn by young James Stewart of Fasnacloich.

I also think that James of the Glen knew all about the conspiracy, though he took no active part in it himself and probably disapproved of any violent reaction to Campbell enmity. Why, then, in order to save his life, did he not turn King's evidence? The answer is simple. He was the 'father' of his clan. And its protector. He gathered all the guilt into himself and allowed his young clansmen to remain alive.

Murder in Lettermore was staged in a marquee at the Duror Festival in July 1951. Outside, the rain and the wind howled insults at a Scottish summer. But inside, a local audience forgot about the weather as the story was told of events which, two hundred years before, had occurred in the surrounding green countryside.

As well as being a 'first' for me, it was also a 'first' for John Cairney, the actor. Still at drama college, he played his first big part – that of Argyll, the presiding judge at the trial – with imagination and astonishing maturity.

I have written about Colin Campbell's murder in some detail because, having been brought up with the thrill of it – at my mother's knee, so to speak – I came to recognize that a thriller with similar question marks was the kind of book I wanted to write.

I also recognize that *Murder in Lettermore* has a kind of affinity with the news stories which today come out of many countries around the world. It tells of political intrigue, of angry young men resorting to violence when tired politicians cease to talk, of authoritarianism refusing to recognize the divinity which resides in every individual. And of a man, who, even in the face of death, can still forgive his enemies and show the way to a happier future.

James Stewart of the Glen was doubtless no saint. But his final words have often helped me to recover a sense of proportion when spite and a desire to do violence (in word if not in deed) threaten to submerge more worthy instincts.

Not long ago I met James MacTaggart on the street in Campbeltown. We talked about James of the Glen and the peculiarly Highland characteristics of the story which appealed to us as Highlanders ourselves. Even as old men we were suddenly excited when the idea sparked between us that we might write a 'musical' based on the tragedy, words by MacVicar, music by MacTaggart.

Then I told James I was writing this book and reminded him of the old days at Kilblaan, when he gave me *The Rudiments of Criticism* and we had discussed poetry into 'the wee sma' 'oors'.

'I'm afraid I never reached your high ideals of writing,' I said.

He laughed. Had there been eyes behind the dark glasses they would have been twinkling. 'I'm afraid I never reached your high ideals of music. But I made my living by it, and you made yours by writing. We can't have been all that bad.'

'Thwarted amateurs?' I said.

He laughed again. He said: 'You could be right at that.'

Index